IN A CLASS OF THEIR OWN

PETER HORSLER

GW00715501

HANBURY PLAYS

**KEEPER'S LODGE
BROUGHTON GREEN
DROITWICH
WORCESTERSHIRE WR9 7EE**

822·914

BY THE SAME AUTHOR:-

One Act
Published by Samuel French
  CHOICE
  CHRISTMAS INCORPORATED
  THE INTRUDERS
Published by Hanbury Plays
  CHRISTMAS WITH MIRABELLE
  TURN THE OTHER CHEEK
  CINDERS ll

Full length
Published by Samuel French
  ON THE VERGE

FIRST PUBLISHED 1985

© Peter Horsler 1985

ISBN 0 907926 73 8

CHARACTERS

Lord Hardcast
Lady Hardcast
Nigel Hardcast - their son
Dolly
Bond
Steward
Mrs. Middy
Chippy

THE TIME IS THE TWENTIETH CENTURY

ACT 1   Sc.1   The Hardcast's country seat. In the beginning.
          Sc.2   The same, a little later on.

ACT 11   Sc.1   The same, much later on.
          Sc.2   The same, later on still.

ACT 111   Sc.1   The same, yet later on still.
          Sc.2   The same, too late.

THE ACTION OF THE PLAY TAKES PLACE IN THE DRAWING ROOM OF THE HARDCAST'S COUNTRY SEAT. U.C. IS A RAISED, RECESSED AREA WITH A GEORGIAN TYPE WINDOW IN ITS L. WALL. WITHIN THIS RECESS, THERE IS A SMALL DRINKS TABLE IN FRONT OF THE GEORGIAN WINDOW AND A TABLE C. WITH A CHAIR EITHER SIDE OF IT. A PAIR OF MATCHING, GEORGIAN STYLE ARCHES, ONE TO THE LEFT AND ONE TO THE RIGHT OF THE RECESS , COMPLETE THE BACK WALL OF THE SET. THE L. ARCH LOOKS OUT ONTO A BALUSTRADE AND FORMAL GARDEN; THE R. REVEALS A HALLWAY THAT LEADS TO THE MAIN PART OF THE HOUSE. IN THE R. WALL OF THE SET IS A LARGE ORNATE FIREPLACE OF UNCERTAIN ORIGIN BELOW WHICH HANGS A CONSPICUOUS BELL PULL. D.L. OF THE SET A DOOR LEADS TO THE SERVANTS' QUARTERS. THE ESSENTIAL FURNITURE, APART FROM THAT ALREADY MENTIONED FOR THE RECESS, IS: A CHAISE LONGUE R.C., A CHAISE LONGUE L.C., A CHAIR D.R. AND A CHAIR D.L. BESIDE WHICH STANDS A SMALL TELEPHONE TABLE. A SMALL MAGAZINE TABLE D.C. MAY PROVE TO BE USEFUL BUT IS NOT ESSENTIAL. THE SET IS DRESSED WITH OLD FAMILY PORTRAITS, THE FAMILY CREST ETC. ALL OF WHICH ARE SURREALISTIC IN STYLE AND THUS ALERT THE AUDIENCE TO THE NATURE OF THE PLAY.

<u>ACT 1   Sc.1.</u>

WHEN THE CURTAIN RISES. LORD HARDCAST IS PERCHED ON HIS SHOOTING STICK IN THE L. ARCHWAY, LOOKING OUT ONTO THE GARDEN. LADY HARDCAST IS SITTING ON THE CHAISE LONGUE R., READING A MAGAZINE AND NIGEL IS LYING FULL-LENGTH ON THE CHAISE LONGUE L., LOOKING AT HIS SHOES WHICH HAVE THE SHOE-LACES UNDONE.

LORD H.   Demned fellah hasn't moved in ten minutes.
LADY H.   Who hasn't, Henry ?
LORD H.   Demned gardener chappie.
LADY H.   You mean Serf.
LORD H.   Fellah's not worth half a sovereign. No good workers left that's the trouble. Same with these lazy, good-for-nothing miners. Dividends not worth a candle. How they expect decent folk to live when they won't work, beats me.

3

LADY H.   The old standards are slipping away, Henry, that's the
    the trouble.
NIGEL   I say, Mater, my shoelaces are undone again. Could you
    tonk the jolly, old bell and save a chap from having to up-end.
LADY H.   (RISING AND PULLING THE BELL CORD D.R.) Really,
    Nigel, it's time you were independent and not expecting your parents
    to see to everything for you.
LORD H.   Demn it, me boy, if I'd asked the mater to ring for a
    servant when I was a lad, the pater would have gone at me with a
    horsewhip.

DOLLY DASHES IN FROM D.L. TO C.

DOLLY   (BREATHLESS) You rang, m'lady ?
LADY H.   I did indeed, Dolly, and it's taken you long enough to get
    here.
DOLLY   Sorry, m'lady, it's them stairs you see -
LADY H.   No, I do not see. Stairs ? Of course there are stairs.
    Servants are always below stairs. Do you expect a room on the ground
    floor ?
DOLLY   Oh, no, m'lady, I know me place. It's just that I can't get
    here no quicker, not wiv them stairs being so narrer.
LADY H.   Of course, if the stairs don't satisfy, if they don't suit,
    there are plenty of young girls who -
DOLLY   I never said they didn't suit, m'lady, honest I never.
LADY H.   Very well then, see to it that next time you don't keep
    us waiting.
DOLLY   Oh, yes, m'lady, I'll practise running up them, I will.
LORD H.   Not fit, Dolly, that's your trouble. Ought to try a few
    route marches, me gel.
DOLLY   I will, m'lord, I will.
LORD H.   In full pack mind. Ask Serf for a few of those big rocks
    he dug up the other week.
DOLLY   Yes, m'lord.
LORD H.   Two on the back and a couple on the chest mind.
LADY H.   Henry !
LORD H.   Sorry, old girl, forgot she was a demned filly.
LADY H.   (TO DOLLY) Well, now you are here, my son needs your
    services.
DOLLY   Oh, m'lady.
NIGEL   (RAISING HIS HAND AND BECKONING HER BUT NOT
    LOOKING ROUND) Come here, Dolly !
DOLLY   (MOVING TIMIDLY ACROSS TO ABOVE CHAISE LONGUE)
    Yes, Master Nigel ?
NIGEL   Mr. Nigel, please, Dolly.
DOLLY   Yes, Mr. Nigel, sir ?
NIGEL   That's better. Now look at me, Dolly.
DOLLY   Look, sir ? Where, sir ?
NIGEL   (POINTING) At me lower extremities, Dolly.

SHE STARES DOWN AT HIS KNEES

NIGEL   Do you see anything amiss ?
DOLLY   No, sir, looks all right to me. Mind you, sir, I ain't no
    judge like.
NIGEL   (WAGGLING HIS FEET) Shoelaces, Dolly, shoelaces.
DOLLY   Oh, shoelaces, Mr. Nigel !

4

NIGEL   Well, tie them, Dolly !
DOLLY   Yes, sir, of course, sir. (SHE TIES THE SHOELACES)
LADY H.   Hurry up, girl ! We haven't got all day. Master Nigel's got
    better things to do than wait for your clumsy fumblings.
NIGEL   Oh, I don't know, Mater.
DOLLY   (CURTSEYING TO LADY H.) Beg pardon, ma'am. Will that
    be all, m'lady ?
LADY H.   For the moment, Dolly.

DOLLY EXITS D.L. BOND ENTERS U.R. AND WHEEZES HIS WAY TO C.

LADY H.   Yes, Bond ?
BOND   Excuse me, m'lady, but will you partake of tea in here or
    shall I -
LORD H.   (PULLING OUT HIS WATCH) Egad, not tea-time is it ?
LADY H.   It's only just gone eleven, Bond ! What can you be thinking
    of ?
BOND   I beg pardon, m'lady, I seem to have lost track of time.
LORD H.   (LOOKING AT HIS WATCH) Fifteen minutes after eleven.
    Not having tea now, are we ?
LADY H.   Of course not, Henry, I'm afraid Bond is a little confused.
BOND   (BACKING D.L.) I beg pardon, m'lady. I hope you'll forgive
    me, m'lady. (HE EXITS AFTER FUMBLING TO FIND THE DOOR D.L.)
LADY H.   I was right, Henry, Bond is past it. What a good job I took
    the precaution of advertising his post. He'll have to go.
LORD H.   (FOLDING UP HIS SHOOTING STICK) Quite right, m'dear,
    quite right. I'll get me gun. (HE EXITS THROUGH THE ARCH U.L.)
LADY H.   Really, Nigel, your father never learns. You'd have thought
    all the trouble we had last time he shot one of the servants -
NIGEL   He means well, Mater.
LADY H.   Yes, of course he does but he should know by now just
    how unreasonable petty officialdom is these days. It doesn't pay to be
    softhearted like your father.
NIGEL   Anyway, Mater, I'm not sure it's the right thing. I mean to
    say, if you were a bit out of sorts, I don't think I'd want to put you
    down, so to speak.
LADY H.   It's not the same thing, Nigel. We're talking about servants
    not about people like ourselves.
NIGEL   Some of the chaps at varsity seem to think there's no
    difference since that Darwin fellah told us we're all descended from
    monkeys.
LADY H.   I'm quite sure, Mr. Darwin didn't mean people like us
    when he said that; he was simply referring to the lower orders.
NIGEL   I daresay you're right, Mater, but these chaps seemed to
    think that the only real difference between them and us is simply a
    question of money and education.
LADY H.   What utter nonsense, Nigel. If that's the level of your
    discussions at Oxford, I think we'd better close the universities down.
    It's all a question of breeding; you wouldn't expect hunters out of shire
    horses, would you ?
NIGEL   No, Mater, but -
LADY H.   Don't go getting ideas below your station, Nigel. And
    while we're on this unsavoury subject, let me say at once, I don't like
    the way you're eyeing young Dolly these days. I know your father thinks
    it's harmless for a young man of the quality to form an amorous
    attachment for a servant gel but I do not.
NIGEL   No, Mater.

LADY H.   Good, so don't let me see you eyeing Dolly in the same way as you should be eyeing the Chumley-Forbington gel. Just because Dolly outwardly resembles a real lady, there is no reason to think they are in any way alike.

NIGEL   No, Mater. Actually, Dolly's a far better looker than the Chumley-Forbington. She squints a bit, don't ya know.

LORD H. ENTERS U.L. CARRYING HIS DOUBLE-BARRELLED SHOTGUN

LADY H.   Don't be coarse, Nigel. You're not your father.

LORD H.   (COMING D. C.) What's that ?

LADY H.   Nothing, Henry.

LORD H.   Have to take poor, old Bond into the wood; can't risk frightening the horses. Wouldn't like Empress to lose her foal.

LADY H.   It's no good, Henry, you can't put poor Bond down. It upsets the local police.

LORD H.   Dash it all, it's a bit orf when a fellah can't help out an old domestic on his own land !

LADY H.   I know just how you feel, dear, but I can't stand the fuss and bother. It'll only give me one of my heads.

NIGEL   Nothing to what it'll do for poor, old Bond.

LADY H.   Quiet, Nigel !

LORD H.   Dash it all, cleaned me gun too.

NIGEL   Why couldn't we put the old chap out to grass, like we do the horses ?

LORD H.   Can't have Bond mooning around the paddock; the horses wouldn't like it.

NIGEL   He could have the hayloft over the stables. We can't turn him out penniless after fifty years.

LADY H.   It's against my principles to be so indulgent, Nigel, but I suppose in this case it could save us quite a bit of bother. What do you say, Henry, shall we be so munificent ?

LORD H.   Suppose so, m'dear. (PATTING HIS GUN) Sure he would have preferred this though. (HE MOVES U.L. PUTS HIS GUN DOWN BY THE FRENCH WINDOWS AND TAKES OFF HIS BINOCULARS)

NIGEL   He'll understand, Pater.

LADY H.   Be extremely grateful, I should hope.

NIGEL   (RISING AND STRETCHING) Homage promised to show me the Rolls. Think I'll breeze over to the garage before lunch. (HE MOVES LACONICALLY TO EXIT U.R.)

LORD H.   Don't go disturbing the hounds now.

NIGEL   Only want to look at the Rolls, Pater.

LADY H.   And remember what I told you, Nigel. Keep away from the servants' quarters !

NIGEL   (STARTLED) What ? Oh, righty ho, Mater. (HE EXITS)

LORD H.   (CROSSING TO U.C. AND PUTTING BINOCULARS INTO CASE ON TABLE IN RECESS) Too demned interested in machines if you ask me. Fellah ought to ride.

LADY H.   I'm afraid it's not horses he's interested in, Henry.

LORD H.   (RETURNING TO U.L. TO PICK UP GUN) More's the pity. Rather tinker with blasted machines.

LADY H.   It's not tinkering with machines that bothers me. It's his unhealthy interest in our servant, Dolly.

LORD H.   (LAUGHING AND CROSSING TO C.) Nothing unhealthy in that, my dear. Why only the other day, old Sir Peregrine was telling me how his young blood, Algernon, took such a shine to the kitchen maids that he had to dismiss three of them in as many months.

6

LADY H.   (RISING AND CROSSING TO RING BELL R.)   Disgusting !
I don't want the bother of breaking in a new maid as well as a butler
but the gel will have to go if she doesn't stop attracting Nigel.
LORD H.   (LAUGHING) Just see the young devil has a cold shower
every morning, what ?
LADY H.   (TURNING TO HIM) Cold showers didn't help you, Henry.
However, we'll deal with that when we have to. At the moment, I'll
tell Bond of our decision.
LORD H.   (SITTING ON U. STAGE END OF R. CHAISE LONGUE)
I hate change but the pack can never stay the same, can it ?

BOND STAGGERS IN D. L.

BOND   (WHEEZING) You rang, m'lady ?
LADY H.   (CROSSING TO C.) Didn't you hear the bell, Bond ?
BOND   I'm sorry, m'lady, the old legs aren't what they were.
LADY H.   It's that we wish to speak to you about, Bond.
BOND   My legs, m'lady ?
LADY H.   Your general slowness, Bond. To say nothing of your
forgetfulness.
BOND   I'm sorry, m'lady, it won't happen again.
LADY H.   (SITTING ON L. CHAISE LONGUE) It won't, Bond, because
we've decided to terminate your employment.
BOND   Very good, m'lady. Will there be anything else ?
LORD H.   What will you do, Bond ?
BOND   (CUPPING HIS HAND TO HIS EAR) What was that, m'lord?
LORD H.   I said what will you do ?
BOND   (LOSING HIS COMPOSURE AND CROSSING TO LORD H'S
LEFT) I don't know, m'lord, I don't know. Please don't concern yourself,
m'lord, I don't want to be any trouble.
LORD H.   There, there, me good fellah. Not my wish, Bond, old
chap. (PATTING HIS GUN) Would like to have done the decent thing.
Had a little patch in mind in the orchard, under the Cox's where we
laid poor, old Grovel, your predecessor. Don't remember him, I suppose ?
BOND   No, m'lord, your father had helped him on before I arrived.
LORD H.   Anyway, Bond, you know how it is these days - pesky
regulations.
BOND   I know, m'lord. Very kind of you to think of me.
LORD H.   (LIFTING THE GUN SO THAT IT POINTS AT BOND'S
HEAD) Long time, fifty years. Would like to show me appreciation.
BOND   (PUSHING THE BARREL AWAY) I quite understand, m'lord,
but you musn't bother yourself. There's always the river.
LADY H.   No, Bond, we've made up our minds. You are to move into
the hayloft over the stables.
BOND   The hayloft ! Oh, m'lady, I'm quite overcome - that you
should think of me - such kindness - I'm sure I don't deserve -
LADY H.   Of course you don't, Bond, but it's just our little gesture.
LORD H.   Mark of our appreciation. Know you can be relied upon not
to disturb the horses.
BOND   Oh, no, m'lord, they won't even know I'm there.
LADY H.   And Cook will save you all her scraps.
BOND   I'm quite overcome, m'lady. When would you wish me to
move ?
LADY H.   When we've found your successor. Don't worry, you'll have
plenty of notice - at least two hours.

7

LORD H. Seeing that you've been with us for fifty years; don't want to rush you, old fellah. Perhaps we could manage half a day. What do you say to that, eh ?

BOND Half a day ! Half a day ! Oh, m'lord, m'lord, m'lord !

BOND BREAKS INTO SOBS

LADY H. (RISING, CROSSING TO FIREPLACE AND PICKING UP FAN) That will do, Bond. You know we can't stand displays of emotion.

LORD H. Not quite the ticket, Bond. Must keep a stiff upper lip, old chap, what ?

LADY H. Don't be ridiculous, Henry, servants don't possess stiff upper lips.

LORD H. What, me dear, no of course not. (HE RISES AND MOVES UP TO THE L. ARCH) As you were, Bond. (HE EXITS)

BOND (SOBBING LOUDER THEN RECOVERING) I beg your pardon m'lady, I can't think what came over me.

LADY H. (RETURNING TO SIT ON R. CHAISE LONGUE. USING FAN) It's all right, Bond. It's all part of your general decrepitude. I understand perfectly.

BOND Yes, m'lady. Thank you, thank you. I'm sure you're right, m'lady.

LORD H. RETURNS WITHOUT HIS GUN AND CROSSES TO TABLE IN RECESS TO RETRIEVE BINOCULARS

LADY H. Naturally, Bond. Now will you please let Homage know that we require the Rolls tomorrow for the point to point.

BOND Yes, m'lady.

LADY H. That'll be all, Bond.

BOND STARTS TO BACK OUT, BOWING OBSEQUIOUSLY

LORD H. (POLISHING HIS BINOCULARS WITH A RED SPOTTED HANKY) Ah, and Bond -

BOND M'lord ?

LORD H. You can use the paddock when the horses are away hunting. (WAVING HANKY FOR EMPHASIS) Canter about, enjoy yourself.

BOND (CRUMBLING) Oh, m'lord, m'lord !

LADY H. Don't set him orf again, Henry. You know I can't bear it.

LORD H. Sorry, m'dear. All right, Bond, orf you go ! At the double !

BOND EXITS D.R. MAKING A FEEBLE ATTEMPT TO OBEY THIS LAST COMMAND.

LORD H. (FEELING IN HIS JACKET POCKET) Demn it !

LADY H. (RISING AND MOVING UP TO THE L. ARCH) I must see what that fool Serf is doing with those bedding plants. The man has no artistic sense at all.

LORD. H. (STILL RUMMAGING IN HIS POCKETS) Demn it ! Must have left me pipe in the library.

LADY H. The library, Henry ? What on earth were you doing in there ?

LORD H. Potting at the rabbits, m'dear, on the croquet lawn.

LADY H. I've asked you not to do that, Henry; it makes the whole room reek of gunpowder.

LORD H. Sorry, m'dear. Got two of the little perishers though.

LADY H. Well, don't do it again. (SHE EXITS CARRYING HER FAN)

8

LORD H.   Very good, m'dear.

HE CONTINUES TO FEEL IN HIS POCKETS. THEN CROSSES TO RING THE BELL. AS HE IS ABOUT TO PULL THE CORD HE CHANGES HIS MIND AND GOES TO EXIT L. BEFORE HE CAN DO SO DOLLY RUSHES IN AND COLLIDES WITH HIM. HE LURCHES TO U.L. SHE SPINS TO D.L.

DOLLY   (AS SHE RUNS IN) No, Master Nigel, no !

NIGEL CHARGES IN AFTER HER AND ALSO COLLIDES WITH LORD H. JUST AS HE IS RECOVERING FROM HIS COLLISION WITH DOLLY.

NIGEL   Whoops ! Sorry, Pater.

LORD H. LOOKS FROM ONE TO THE OTHER, COMPREHENSION OF THE SITUATION SLOWLY DAWNING UPON HIM.
LORD H.   What the - ? Oh, oh ! (LAUGHING) Carry on, me boy, carry on. (HE EXITS L.)
NIGEL   (MOVING SLOWLY DOWN TO HER) Just one kiss, Dolly, just one.
DOLLY   Please, Master Nigel, you'll get me fired you will, chasing me like that.
NIGEL   (PURSUING HER) You shouldn't have walked past the garage and shown me your servant's quarters, Dolly.
DOLLY   (RETREATING BEFORE HIM) I'm sure I did no such thing, Master Nigel. I'd been down to the post office to phone my mother. She's very poorly you see and -
NIGEL   All I can see, Dolly, is a delectable, young filly who's longing for a chap to mount her. (HE GRABS HER)
DOLLY   (STRUGGLING) Stop it ! Stop it ! Please, Master Nigel, what's to become of me if her ladyship finds out ? (SHE SOBS AND STOPS STRUGGLING)
NIGEL   (PUTTING HIS ARM ROUND HER) She won't find out, Dolly, I promise you. She's gone to the gardens.
DOLLY   Oh, Master Nigel.
NIGEL   (GUIDING HER TO THE CHAISE LONGUE) Now you just lie down here 'till you feel better.
DOLLY   On her ladyship's sofa ? I couldn't !
NIGEL   (PUSHING HER DOWN) Of course you could. Just for a minute.
DOLLY   Oh, Master Nigel, you're so kind.
NIGEL   I am, aren't I ? (HE PUSHES HER DOWN KISSING HER)
DOLLY   Master Nigel, Master Nigel, oh - Mr. Nigel !

LADY H. ENTERS U.L. SHE IS STILL HOLDING HER FAN

LADY H.   That fool, Serf, has gone orf to collect manure. I just couldn't be bothered to - (SHE SEES NIGEL AND DOLLY ON THE CHAISE LONGUE) Good gracious, Nigel, what on earth are you doing ?

NIGEL LEAPS UP AND RUSHES TO ABOVE CHAISE LONGUE

NIGEL   It's - it's Dolly, Mater !
LADY H.   I can see that !
NIGEL   She's fainted and I'm trying to bring her round.
DOLLY   (STRUGGLING TO HER FEET) I'm sorry, m'lady. I was just doing some dusting when I come over all faint. It's the bad news; about me mother that is.
LADY H.   This simply will not do, Dolly. Bad news or no, fainting on my chaise longue is a liberty I cannot condone under any circumstances.

9

DOLLY   (BACKING DOWN L. TRYING TO MAKE HER ESCAPE)
No, m'lady, I'm terribly sorry, your ladyship.

LADY H.   As for you, Nigel, I simply will not have you interfering
with the servants, especially when they are not well. (SHE FLICKS THE
CHAISE LONGUE WITH HER FAN) You never know what you might
catch. (SHE SITS) However, I shall overlook it this time, Dolly, but in
future, if I find you on the furniture, no matter what the pretext, it
will mean instant dismissal. Do you understand ?

DOLLY   (CROSSING TO LADY H'S R.) Yes, m'lady. Beg pardon,
m'lady, but as my mother's so ill, could you see your way to lettin' me
have me half-day this week. I know it's not the third week of the
month but she really is poorly, your ladyship, and I can't rest 'till I've
seen she's all right wiv me own eyes.

LADY H.   Well really, child. I have just excused your inexcusable
behaviour and here you are asking for favours.

DOLLY   I know, m'lady, I'm sorry but she really is ever so poorly.

NIGEL   If you were ever so poorly, Mater, I should jolly well want
to come and see you.

LADY H.   Be quiet, Nigel. You know nothing about domestics.

NIGEL   I was learning, Mater, when you -

LADY H.   And what have you learned, Nigel ?

NIGEL   Not to interfere, Mater.

LORD H. APPEARS AT THE ARCH U.L.

LADY H.   Good, so kindly go away.

NIGEL DRIFTS UP TO LORD H.'S R.

LADY H.   Well, Dolly, I'm sure your filial concern does you credit
but this is a serious matter and one to consider carefully.(SHE PONDERS
ON DOLLY'S REQUEST)

NIGEL   (TO LORD H.) I say, Pater, I ran into old Goofy Hunter
last week and, what do ya know, his pater's bought him a ripping, little,
private aeroplane. Absolute winner, he says it is - tremendous fun.
Couldn't see your way clear, I suppose, to supplement the old allowance,
sort of advance, could you ?

LORD H. MOVES DOWN TO SIT ON D.S. END OF L. CHAISE LONGUE

LADY H.   No, Dolly, on reflection, I'm afraid I can't allow you to
change your afternoon off. If your mother is foolish enough to become
ill in a week when you have no time off, I cannot be expected to alter
my arrangements to suit.

DOLLY   No, m'lady.

LORD H.   Not a good time, me boy, dividends down and all that.
How much would the infernal thing cost, do ya think ?

NIGEL   (COMING DOWN TO LORD H'S R.) About four hundred
pounds, Pater.

LORD H. PONDERS ON THIS

LADY H.   It's no good you standing there looking sullen, Dolly. Let
me remind you that a great many gels would give their right arms for
a position worth forty pounds a year.

LORD H.   Lot of money, four hundred pounds.

LADY H.   Forty pounds is a good wage for a maid, I can tell you.

LORD H.   Lot of money, four hundred pounds for an infernal machine.

LADY H.   And remember you only do sixteen hours a day.

LORD H.   And remember, it represents six months rent on the tied cottages.

DOLLY   Please, m'lady, I'll never ask another favour and I'll give up all me half days for the next six months.

NIGEL   Please, Pater, I'll sell me racing car and two of the motor bikes.

LADY H.   I have said no, Dolly, so let that be the end of the matter. Not another word, is that clear ?

LORD H.   Well, old chap, like a fellah with a spirit of adventure. Now cut along and order the dratted thing before I change me mind.

NIGEL   Thanks, Pater. (HE DASHES OFF U.R. PINCHING DOLLY'S BOTTOM AS HE PASSES ABOVE HER)

LADY H.   Away with you, girl, about your work !

DOLLY   (CURTSEYING AND MOVING TO EXIT D.L.) Yes, m'lady.

LADY H.   And, Dolly ?

DOLLY   Yes, m'lady ?

LADY H.   We shall be away tomorrow at the point to point so I shall expect you to report to Mrs. Middy every two hours. Is that understood?

DOLLY   Yes, m'lady. (SHE EXITS)

LADY H.   Really, Henry, I don't know what things are coming to.

LORD H.   Standards not what they were, me dear. In the pater's day we never had to think of servants as people. Never had any trouble in the good, old days.

LADY H.   We're too indulgent, Henry, that's the trouble. I sometimes think we're guilty of anthropomorphism.

LORD H.   Eh? Oh - suppose we are, m'dear. Can't take liberties with the hounds either. Got to show 'em who's boss right from the start.

MRS. MIDDY ENTERS U.R. AND COMES D. TO LADY H'S R.

MRS. MIDDY   Excuse me, m'lady, but there's a man who says he's come about the butler's job. I've told him he must have got the wrong address but he says he's not going until I inform your ladyship that he's here.

LADY H.   That's quite all right, Mrs. Middy. I was expecting him.

MRS. MIDDY   Oh, I didn't know Mr. Bond was leaving, your ladyship.

LORD H.   Not surprising, fellah didn't know himself 'till a few minutes ago.

MRS. MIDDY   Oh, I see, your lordship. Very good, your ladyship, I'll send him up. (SHE EXITS U.R.)

LADY H.   I doubt he'll do, Henry. It's almost impossible to find servants with the right attitude these days.

LORD H.   (RISING AND MOVING UP TO THE ARCH U.L.) Always a demned problem, butlers. Look here, m'dear, if you're going to see this chappie, I think I'll toddle off to the stables. Never could judge servants; better with horses, what ?

LADY H.   I wish you'd take more interest in household matters, Henry. If you can judge a good mare, surely servants should be no problem.

LORD H.   Not the same thing, m'dear. These days servants ask questions. Sooner talk to old Empress. (HE EXITS U.L.)

MRS MIDDY ENTERS U.R. FOLLOWED BY STEWARD WHO IS WEARING A DARK OVERCOAT OVER HIS BUTLER'S SUIT AND IS CARRYING A BOWLER HAT.

MRS. MIDDY   Mr. Steward, your ladyship.

MRS. MIDDY CURTSEYS AND IMMEDIATELY EXITS D.L.

LADY H.   Well, come in, man, let's have a look at you !

STEWARD MOVES OBSEQUIOUSLY TO C.

LADY H.   (RISING AND WALKING AROUND HIM) Hmm. (SHE FEELS HIS ARM MUSCLES) Hmm. (OPENING HIS MOUTH AND LOOKING AT HIS TEETH) How old are you, Stuart ?
STEWARD   (SPEAKING WITH DIFFICULTY) Steward, your ladyship.
LADY H.   I asked how old you are. Are you deaf ?
STEWARD   Fortyish, m'lady.
LADY H.   Fortyish. Hmm. (SHE PRODS HIS MIDRIFF) Well, should have a bit of wind left then. (POINTING AT CHAIR D.L.) Sit down, Stuart !
STEWARD   Sit, your ladyship ?
LADY H.   This once, yes. Of course, if I employ you, you will never sit in my presence again but for the purpose of this interview, I require you to sit so please to do so. (SHE POINTS AT L. CHAISE LONGUE, CROSSES TO FIREPLACE AND PUTS FAN ON MANTLESHELF)

STEWARD MOVES GINGERLY TO THE L. CHAISE LONGUE AND SITS. LADY H. CROSSES TO TELEPHONE TABLE AND PICKS UP CIGARETTE BOX

LADY H.   Now, Stuart, I want you to feel completely at ease.
STEWARD   The name is Steward, m'lady. (SPELLING IT) S.t.e.w.a.r.d.
LADY H.   I prefer 'Stuart'. (EASING UP BEHIND L. CHAISE LONGUE) However, I shall not insist on you changing it by deed poll as we are a very liberal family; a fact, I might say, that is not always in our best interests. No I'm afraid our liberalism is often mistaken for weakness by the lower orders. Some of our servants have exploited our kindnesses most shamefully.
STEWARD   How dreadful, your ladyship. You make me ashamed of my own class. But I'm sure such behaviour never came from anyone with the rank of butler.
LADY H.   That of course would be unthinkable. (SHE OFFERS HIM A CIGARETTE) Cigarette ?
STEWARD   Oh, no thank you, m'lady, I don't smoke and even if I did, I could never do so in your ladyship's presence.

LADY H. RETURNS THE CIGARETTE BOX TO THE TELEPHONE TABLE THEN CIRCLES ABOVE L. CHAISE LONGUE IN THE MANNER OF THE STEREOTYPE INTERROGATOR

LADY H.   I am gratified to hear that, Stuart. Now, you have been in the service of Lady Grindthorpe for the last seven years ?
STEWARD   Yes, m'lady.
LADY H.   You have references of course ?
STEWARD   (TAKING TWO BROWN ENVELOPES FROM HIS POCKET) From my last two positions, your ladyship. Before that I was only the pantry boy.
LADY H.   (TAKING THE ENVELOPES) I see. I shall read these when I have formed my own opinion. (SUDDENLY) Why did you leave Lady Grindthorpe ?
STEWARD   I - I wished to work in a larger establishment, for the real quality, m'lady.
LADY H.   (BRINGING HER FACE CLOSE TO HIS) They didn't connect you with the stolen silver then ?
STEWARD   (ALARMED) Stolen silv -
LADY H.   (WAVING THE ENVELOPES) Don't think these forgeries fool me. You're nothing but a little sneak thief ! Why don't you admit it? Nothing will be said outside this room.

12

STEWARD   But, m'lady, I know nothing about any silver.

LADY H.   Or Lord Grindthorpe's gold hunter ?

STEWARD   No, m'lady, I swear -

LADY H.   (DROPPING HER INTERROGATION VOICE AND CROSSING
L. TO PUT LETTERS ON TABLE) And that's another thing, Stuart, I
will not have my staff swearing.

STEWARD   Truly, your ladyship, as God's my witness, I had no idea
that Lady Grindthorpe had lost her silver.

LADY H.   (CROSSING BELOW STEWARD TO C.) Well, I don't suppose
she has, Stuart, but one has to make these little tests, doesn't one. Just
one of my amusing little games, Stuart. Both Lord Hardcast and myself
have strong senses of humour. I hope you're not one of those dour sort
of people who cannot take a joke.

STEWARD   (FORCING A WEAK SMILE) Oh, indeed not, your ladyship.
I hope I can see the funny side of things.

LADY H.   It's what gives life its light and shade, eh, Stuart ?

STEWARD   Indubitably, your ladyship. (HE FORCES A LAUGH)

THEY LAUGH TOGETHER

LADY H.   (SUDDENLY) Mind you, I will not tolerate jokes against
the family.

STEWARD   Such profanity is unthinkable, your ladyship.

LADY H.   Good, Stuart, my sentiments exactly. (SHE CROSSES TO
THE FIREPLACE AND TAKES A   HATPIN FROM AN ORNAMENTAL
BOX ON THE MANTLESHELF) Now, one further thing. (HOLDING UP
THE HATPIN AND MOVING TOWARDS HIM) Do you know   what this is,
Stuart ?

STEWARD   (PEERING) It would appear to be a hatpin, your ladyship.

LADY H.   Quite right, Stuart, quite right ! (SHE LUNGES FORWARD
AND JABS THE PIN INTO HIS LEG)

STEWARD   (GRASPING HIS LEG) Ooh - oh - ooh ! (RECOVERING HIS
COMPOSURE) I humbly beg your ladyship's pardon. I'm very much afraid
that I have inadvertently put my leg in the way of your ladyship's pin.
I can't imagine how I could have been so clumsy. I hope your ladyship
will overlook this momentary lapse of mine.

LADY H.   (RETURNING THE HATPIN TO THE FIREPLACE)   Not at
all, Stuart, not at all. Think no more of it.

STEWARD   Very magnaminous of your ladyship.

LADY H.   (RETURNING TO C.) Well, that all seems very satisfactory.
Could you start today ?

STEWARD   If it pleases your ladyship.

LADY H.   Good. Shall we say then that you will take over your
duties in time for dinner this evening.

STEWARD   I shall be honoured, your ladyship.

LADY H.   And, Stuart ?

STEWARD   M'lady ?

LADY H.   Have the goodness not to sit in my presence.

STEWARD   (RISING) I beg your ladyship's pardon.

LADY H.   I shall overlook it this once. Now, perhaps, you would be
good enough to arrange for your things to be taken to your room.

STEWARD   (BOWING AND MOVING U.R. Thank you, m'lady.

LADY H.   And, Stuart ?

STEWARD   M'lady ?

LADY H.   Kindly use the servants' door and inform Mrs. Middy that
Bond's belongings are to be taken over to the stables.

13

STEWARD   (CROSSING TO D.L. TURNING AND BOWING) Very good, your ladyship. (HE EXITS D.L. CLOSING THE DOOR AFTER HIM)

LADY H. CROSSES TO THE TABLE L. PICKS UP THE ENVELOPES THAT STEWARD GAVE HER TOGETHER WITH THE PAPER KNIFE AND MOVES BACK TO SIT ON THE CHAISE LONGUE L.

LORD HARDCAST ENTERS U.L.

LORD H.   No demned good, I suppose ?

LADY H.   On the contrary, Henry, he passed the subservience test with flying colours. The man's engaged. (SHE SLITS OPEN ONE OF THE ENVELOPES His name is Stuart. (SPELLING IT OUT) S.t.u.a.r.t. (SHE SLITS OPEN THE OTHER ENVELOPE ON THE LAST 'T' OF STUART AS THE CURTAIN FALLS)

ACT 1 Sc.2.

THE SAME. A LITTLE LATER ON. WHEN THE CURTAIN RISES DOLLY IS DUSTING THE TABLE U.R. IN THE RECESS. SHE FLICKS IT OVER WITH A FEATHER DUSTER AND THEN MOVES D. TO THE FIREPLACE. AS SHE DOES SO MRS. MIDDY ENTERS U.R. CONSULTING A NOTE BOOK. SHE CROSSES TO C.

MRS. MIDDY   Have you any idea, child,   why Mr. Steward has called a meeting in her ladyship's drawing room ?

DOLLY   No, ma'am.

MRS. MIDDY   I thought there must be something amiss with the room; something to which he wished to draw our attention but I can see nothing out of place.

DOLLY   Don't think it has anything to do with the room, ma'am. It's ter do with this new union he's always on about. Least, that's what I reckon.

MRS. MIDDY   Are you telling me he's dared to call all the servants together in her ladyship's private quarters for a purpose that has nothing to do with her ladyship's welfare ?

DOLLY   Only what I reckons, ma'am.

MRS. MIDDY   (SITTING ON THE L. CHAISE LONGUE) Well, if that's the case, it's an unforgivable liberty and I feel it my solemn duty to stay and report all that transpires to her ladyship. And, what is more, I shall inform Mr. Steward of my intentions. Oh, do stop flapping about with that duster; you're doing more harm than good. And for goodness sake, sit down !

DOLLY   (STOPPING AND MOVING QUICKLY TO C.) Ooh, I daren't do that, ma'am. Her ladyship said I'd get the boot if she caught me on the furniture.

MRS. MIDDY   Her ladyship isn't here and until she is, I am in charge of what happens in this house. So do as I tell you and sit down !

DOLLY   Yes, ma'am. Where, ma'am ?

MRS. MIDDY   (POINTING TO THE R. CHAISE LONGUE There, girl !

DOLLY   (SITTING HESITATINGLY) Don't seem right somehow.

MRS. MIDDY   It isn't right and I shall demand a full explanation from Mr. Steward when he has the goodness to put in an appearance.

DOLLY   (PAUSING AND FIDGETING NERVOUSLY) Ma'am ?
MRS. MIDDY   What now ?
DOLLY   When do you think her ladyship will be back ?
MRS. MIDDY   Goodness knows. All depends on whether they come straight back here from the races or go visiting. Could be midnight or any time now.
DOLLY   (JUMPING UP AND RUNNING TO DOOR D.L.) Ooh - er !
MRS. MIDDY   Sit down ! We shall get plenty of warning when they come; so sit down !

DOLLY SITS APPREHENSIVELY IN CHAIR D.L. STEWARD ENTERS D.L. HE IS CARRYING A CLIPBOARD AND CROSSES BRISKLY TO C.

STEWARD   (TICKING A LIST WITH A PENCIL) Now, I've seen Serf, Homage before he left, both grooms, the stable boy, Doris, Margaret and Mrs. Pottage.
MRS. MIDDY   (RISING) Mr. Steward, I really must protest ! Cook and the maids come under my jurisdiction.
STEWARD   (IGNORING HER) That leaves just Dolly and the old biddy. (LOOKING UP) Ah, there you are. Good.
MRS. MIDDY   It is not good at all, Mr. Steward. I demand an explanation.
STEWARD   Well, Serf wouldn't come on account of his boots; Cook's in the middle of baking; Homage has taken them to the races; Doris is laid up; Margaret's -
MRS. MIDDY   I do not mean why the staff are not here.
STEWARD   No ?
MRS. MIDDY   No. I want to know why we have been summoned to her ladyship's drawing room ?
STEWARD   I just thought it would be a nice venue for our first meeting, that's all.
MRS. MIDDY   You thought - ?
STEWARD   (MOVING UP TO TABLE IN RECESS AND PUTTING NOTES DOWN) Just the right setting for what I have to say.
MRS. MIDDY   (RISING AND MOVING TO STEWARD'S L.) I don't think there's any need for you to make a speech, Mr. Steward, since there are only two of us. Using her ladyship's room in this way; it's absolutely disgraceful !
STEWARD   Not make a speech ? Of course, I've got to make a speech. It's in the union's procedures for meetings. Besides, I've got it all prepared.
MRS. MIDDY   Very well, Mr. Steward, make it if you must but I warn you, I shall make notes on everything you say and shall report it to her ladyship the moment she returns.
DOLLY   I bet you make lovely speeches, Mr. Stuart.
STEWARD   The name's Steward, Dolly.
DOLLY   They don't call you that though, do they ?
STEWARD   They will, Dolly, they will.
MRS. MIDDY   You mind what you say, girl, or I shall report on your attitude too.
DOLLY   Ooh, ma'am, I'm sure I -
STEWARD   (POINTING AT MRS M.) That's just an example, brothers, just one example among hundreds, of the sort of intimidation practised on our members.
DOLLY   (TO MRS. MIDDY) Who's he talking to ?
MRS. MIDDY   I hope you're not addressing me, Mr. Steward, as 'brother'!
STEWARD   Brothers, sisters, we are all in one movement now; a movement destined to bring justice to the oppressed.

MRS. MIDDY   I object to being called 'sister' too, Mr. Steward !
STEWARD   (PICKING UP HIS NOTES AND ADDRESSING AUDIENCE AT LARGE) A movement now in its infancy but soon to wield such power that the greedy gentry who feed on the sweat of us servants -
DOLLY   Ooh - er !
STEWARD   - will be forced to their knees to listen to our demands. It will be a new (CONSULTING HIS NOTES) mill - mill - millenium. 'Injustice' will be an obsolete word. The lord will sit down with the groom; the lady with the parlour-maid -
DOLLY   Ooh - er !
STEWARD   Equality will have been achieved. (POINTING AT DOLLY) You, Dolly, will take tea with her ladyship.
DOLLY   Go on !
MRS. MIDDY   What rubbish !
DOLLY   You mean I'll be as good as her ladyship, Mr. Steward ?
STEWARD   Equal, yes, Dolly. No worse; no better.
DOLLY   That's silly, that is. She's one of the grand folk and me -
MRS. MIDDY   You're just a nobody, Dolly, but a very lucky girl to have a position at all.
STEWARD   Lucky ? It's the Hardcasts what's lucky ! Not for much longer though, eh, Dolly ?
MRS. MIDDY   Stop filling her head with nonsense, Steward. You'll give the girl ideas that will get her into trouble.
STEWARD   I want to get her into trouble, Mrs. Middy.
DOLLY   Ooh, ooh, then what'll become of me ?
STEWARD   (CROSSING TO DOLLY) I want to get you into trouble, Dolly, so the union can get you out; show 'em what a union's about, won't it ? Standing up for your rights is going to mean trouble. (HE CROSSES ABOVE L. CHAISE LONGUE TO C.) but if you don't want to be a downtrodden work-slave, it has to be faced.
MRS. MIDDY   All you'll succeed in doing, Steward, is getting everyone dismissed. Where will your precious union be then ?
STEWARD   (COMING D. TO R. OF MRS. MIDDY) That's where you're wrong, Mrs. Middy, that's the power of the union: sticking together, one for all; all for one - one out, all out.
MRS. MIDDY   What nonsense. They could replace the lot of us any time they like. Even you must know that.
STEWARD   No, Mrs. Middy, oh no. The union does not operate just in this house but joins all the workers in all the big houses together. If they fire us, there's not a servant in the country who'll work for them. And you tell me where they'll be then, eh ? They're helpless without us: her ladyship can't cook, sew, clean, organise the running of the house; his lordship can do nothing except shoot, fish and hunt and as for their son, Nigel, he can't even tie his own shoelaces. They're as helpless as children; they depend on us far more than we depend on them.
DOLLY   Could I really be a lady, Mr. Steward, live in a big house, wear lovely clothes, ride in a real motor car ?
STEWARD   Of course you could, Dolly. And you shall - through the power of the union.
MRS. MIDDY   (RISING) Mr. Steward, this nonsense has gone far enough. (SHE PUSHES HIM SO THAT HE SITS ON THE CHAISE LONGUE L. AND THEN SHE MOVES UP TO THE RAISED SECTION OF THE RECESS WHERE SHE PROCEEDS TO MAKE A SPEECH TO THE AUDIENCE) Ladies and gentlemen -
DOLLY   (STANDING AND POINTING AT STEWARD) There's only him and me.

16

STEWARD   (PULLING HER DOWN TO SIT BESIDE HIM) We represent the masses, Dolly.

MRS. MIDDY   Please don't interrupt ! You've had your say. Ladies and gentlemen, I thank God daily that I belong to an old, established country that does not heed the rantings and ravings of revolutionaries. We all know, don't we, that our society, like nature, is made according to God's will and that He, in his wisdom, has ordained that there shall be the high and the low among us.

STEWARD   And those in the middle, enjoying the best of both worlds. (HE NUDGES DOLLY AND LAUGHS. ON HIS SECOND NUDGE SHE JOINS IN RELUCTANTLY)

MRS. MIDDY   If you interrupt again, I shall - I shall -

STEWARD   What ? Report me to your union ? (HE APPLAUDS, NUDGING DOLLY TO JOIN IN. STOPPING) You see, Mrs. Middy, if labour is not organised, it is helpless. Eh, Dolly ? (HE CLAPS AGAIN)

DOLLY   Oh, right, Mr. Steward.

MRS. MIDDY   Mr. Steward, will you stop referring to me as 'labour' !

STEWARD   (MOVING AGGRESSIVELY TOWARDS HER AND PUSHING HER DOWN TO SIT BESIDE DOLLY) Well, that's what you are, like it or not. Oh, I know you think you're superior to Dolly and the rest of them but you're not: you're selling yourself just as much as they are.

MRS. MIDDY   Mr. Steward !

STEWARD   You don't want change because you're frightened you'll end being classed with Mrs. Pottage, Doris and the others. Right, Dolly?

DOLLY   Oh, right, Mr. Steward.

STEWARD   You're ashamed of being thought working class, that's your trouble. So what do you do ? You try and ape the gentry. But I'll tell you this: if you side with them against us, you won't find yourself comfortably in the middle like you are now. Oh, no, you'll be abandoned, isolated, an outcast from both camps. Right, Dolly ?

DOLLY   Right, Mr. Steward.

STEWARD   Hands up who's going to join then. (PAUSE) I said hands up all of them what's going to join !

DOLLY RAISES HER HAND

MRS. MIDDY   Join you ? I'd rather die !

STEWARD   (GIVING HER A PAMPHLET) Well read this before you do.

MRS. MIDDY   (TAKING THE PAMPHLET AS IF IT HAD AN OFFENSIVE SMELL AND READING) "Charter for the Workers" (TOSSING IT TO THE FLOOR) A fig for your leaflet, Mr. Steward ! "Charter for the Workers"! It's nothing short of blasphemy !

THERE IS THE SOUND OF A CAR APPROACHING ON A GRAVEL DRIVE

Good gracious, her ladyship's back ! Make yourself scarce, Mr. Steward, or you'll be packing your bags. (SWEEPING DOWN L.) Come, Dolly, you will have to work late tonight to make up for the time that this fool has made you lose. (SHE EXITS)

DOLLY WHO HAS BEEN FROZEN TO THE SEAT AT THE SOUND OF THE CAR RUSHES TO FOLLOW HER

STEWARD   (STOPPING DOLLY AT THE DOOR) Make up your own mind, girl. It won't be easy, Dolly, but it's now or never.

DOLLY   Ooh, I don't know, Mr. Steward, I'm all of a doodah !

STEWARD   (TAKING HER ARM) Come along to my pantry and take the pledge - you'll never look back, my girl. (THEY EXIT D.L.)

LADY HARDCAST, LORD HARDCAST AND NIGEL ENTER U.R. LADY HARDCAST MOVES DOWN TO THE L. CHAISE LONGUE WHILE LORD HARDCAST CROSSES ABOVE THE R. CHAISE LONGUE AND DOWN TO THE CHAIR D.L. NIGEL FOLLOWS LADY HARDCAST ON BUT STAYS UP IN THE ARCHWAY

LADY H.   (AS SHE ENTERS) What a simply dreadful day. I don't know when I felt so exhausted. What is the world coming to ? That hateful fellow, Homage, refusing to drive us home because he had been working for a mere sixteen hours. How dare servants tell us when they should stop work. Really, I had no choice but to dismiss him on the spot. If Nigel hadn't driven the Rolls, I don't know how we should have got home.

LORD H.   Jolly good show, me boy.

NIGEL   Super fun, chauffeuring.

LADY H.   Don't tell me you enjoyed doing servants' work, Nigel.

NIGEL   (COMING C.) But I did, Mater. I find I quite like doing things. You won't believe this but I tried tying my shoelaces this morning and I found it was not so jolly difficult either; made a pretty fair stab at it. (SITTING ON R. CHAISE LONGUE) Only snag was, I fell over when I tried to stand up because I'd tied both shoes together.

LADY H.   Nigel, I despair of ever making a gentleman of you.

LORD H.   Never keep a dog and bark yourself, me boy.

NIGEL   Anyway, it was great fun, driving the Rolls, except when we went through that red traffic light.

LADY H.   Do you know, Henry, I believe that wretched policeman was about to book us for that if I hadn't told him quite forcibly who we were.

LORD H.   That settled the blighter, what ?

LADY H.   I should hope so.

LORD H.   Jolly soon turned his attention to that fool of a salesman we ran into.

NIGEL   Well, to be absolutely fair, Pater, we were crossing a red light.

LORD H.   Stupid, little twerp should have seen us coming, shouldn't he ? Rolls is big enough, ain't it ?

NIGEL   Still, hardly fair to nab him for dangerous driving; was my fault ya know.

LORD H.   Nonsense, me boy, you're a Hardcast.

LADY H.   Something you seem inclined to forget, Nigel. Always remember who you are. Stop tying your shoelaces and stay upright.

LORD H.   There were Hardcasts at Agincourt, me boy, always remember that.

LADY H.   Let's hope they didn't wear shoelaces. Since you like doing things, Nigel, perhaps you'd ring for tea before I expire. Oh, that detestable Homage !

NIGEL RINGS FOR SERVICE. LORD H. OPENS THE PAPER THAT HE HAS BROUGHT WITH HIM

LADY H.   Nigel, it was clever of you to drive us home but I hope in future you're not going to dirty your hands fiddling with oily engines and things like that. Not quite the thing, you know.

NIGEL   (RETURNING TO SIT ON CHAISE LONGUE R.) Just a hobby, Mater, that I think I'll take up.

LADY H.   A very unsuitable one for a Hardcast, Nigel.

LORD H.   (STARING AT HIS PAPER) Great Scot !

LADY H.	Bad news, Henry ?
LORD H.	Catastrophic, absolute disaster !
NIGEL	Stock exchange burnt down has it ?
LORD H.	No worse, far worse !
LADY H.	The Chumley-Forbington gel's engaged ?
LORD H.	No, no, - rain stopped play !
LADY H.	That's a relief.
LORD H.	Dash it all, woman, we were winning !
LADY H.	Don't call me a 'woman', Henry !

LORD H. Sorry, m'dear. (PUZZLED) You are one though ? I mean, I seem to remember -

LADY H. You know perfectly well, Henry, I will not tolerate you addressing me in that coarse manner.

LORD H. Sorry, m'dear, a fellah forgets himself when he's provoked, what ?

A HORSE NEIGHS LOUDLY IN THE GARDEN OUTSIDE

(JUMPING UP) What the blazes ! That's Empress ! (HE RUSHES TO THE FRENCH WINDOW) Spluttering fetlocks, she's eating the roses !

LADY H. (JUMPING UP AND JOINING HIM AT THE WINDOW) What can that oaf, Serf, be thinking of !

LORD H. (CROSSING TO RING THE BELL) It'll be that old fool, Bond, I'll be bound, loose in the paddock - enough to frighten any horse!

LADY H. Where is Serf ? Where are all the servants ?

LORD H. (RUSHING OFF U.L.) Got to catch her; valuable mare.

DOLLY ENTERS DOWN LEFT

DOLLY M'lady ?

LADY H. (SWEEPING D.C.) Dolly ! Where have you been, girl ? How dare you keep us waiting like this ! I've a good mind to dismiss you instantly, do you hear ?

DOLLY You can't dismiss me, m'lady.

LADY H. (THUNDERSTRUCK) What !

DOLLY Beggin' yer ladyship' pardon but Mr. Steward says if anyone is victimised, it'll make the strike much worse.

LADY H. Strike !!

DOLLY (MOVING TO LADY H. Yes, ma'am, we're all out on account of Mr. Homage. I've not come 'cause you rang, ma'am but to tell you that Mr. Steward is willing to negotiate. 'Course, you'll have to give poor Mr. Homage his job back first but he thinks, Mr. Steward that is, ma'am, that a settlement - whatever that is - can be reached. That's what I was to tell yer, ma'am.

LADY H. (REELING BACK TO COLLAPSE ON R. CHAISE LONGUE) Settlement !! Nigel, I'm about to faint. Pour me a brandy !

NIGEL RISES AND MOVES UP TO THE DRINKS TABLE U.C. LADY H. TOTTERS UP BEHIND HIM AND PUSHES HIM ASIDE

Never mind, I'll do it myself !

NIGEL (BREAKING D. TO FIREPLACE) I say, Dolly, that was jolly plucky. Makes a fellah see a girl in a new light, what ?

DOLLY (CROSSING TO NIGEL) It's all for one and one for all now, Mr. Nigel.

NIGEL 'The Three Musketeers', eh, Dolly ?

DOLLY Don't know about them, sir. It's what Mr. Steward says. (TO LADY H.) What am I to tell Mr. Steward then, ma'am ?

LADY H.   (PUTTING DOWN HER GLASS AND COMING DOWN TO DOLLY'S L.) I'll tell you what to tell Mr. Stuart, Dolly. (SHE PICKS UP HER PARASOL FROM THE L. CHAISE LONGUE WHERE SHE HAD PLACED IT ON HER RETURN FROM THE RACES AND HANGS IT ON DOLLY'S L. ARM) Tell him that he is dismissed instantly. (GIVING DOLLY HER HAT) Tell him you are all dismissed instantly. (GIVING DOLLY HER GLOVES AND THEN SWEEPING DOWN TO OPEN THE DOOR D.L.) Tell him if he is not off my property within one hour, I will have him and all the rest of you arrested for trespass. Is that clear?

DOLLY   (LOSING HER COMPOSURE) Oh, m'lady, you don't mean- but, me lady -

LADY H.   (IMPERIOUSLY) Go, girl, deliver the message !

DOLLY   (BURSTING INTO TEARS AND RUSHING OUT D.L.) Yes, m'lady.

LADY H.   (CLOSING THE DOOR AFTER HER) Wretched child, she's so easily led. (SHE MOVES TO THE PHONE)

NIGEL   Not all that easily, Mater, actually.

LADY H. PICKS UP THE PHONE. NIGEL DRIFTS ACROSS, PICKS UP A MAGAZINE FROM THE TABLE C. AND LIES DOWN ON THE L. CHAISE LONGUE. HE READS DURING LADY H'S PHONE CALL)

LADY H.   (PICKING UP THE PHONE) I must ring Marjorie. The Grindthorpes are always over-staffed. I'm sure she can loan me a few to tide me over. (SPEAKING INTO THE PHONE) This is Lady Hardcast. I want to speak to Lady Marjorie. What ? Lady Marjorie Grindthorpe of Grindthorpe Hall of course ! (TO NIGEL) The ignorance of these Post Office people is simply staggering. (ANSWERING THE PHONE) What ? No, I don't know the number ! It's your business to know numbers I should think. (TO NIGEL) This girl will have to be reported to the Postmaster general. (SITTING AND SPEAKING INTO PHONE) Hello, Marjorie ? At last. My dear, the time they've taken to put me through to you. Listen, dear, we're in the most awful trouble: the servants have all gone stark, staring mad. No, I don't know why, dear, but I suspect it might have something to do with the bromide that Henry insists on putting in their tea. Anyway, I've had to dismiss the lot. Yes, the lot, dear ! Terribly inconvenient; so I'm hoping you could loan me the odd maid or two and your assistant cook. I shall have to put up with that old fool, Bond, again for a few weeks but it can't be helped. Have I what, dear ? (RISING) Negotiated a settlement ! Good heavens ! You don't mean ? You have ? The only way out ? Well, really, Marjorie, I would have thought you'd have more spunk ! Spunk, dear ! No, no, it doesn't matter. Give my regards to Horatio. (SHE PUTS DOWN THE PHONE AND SLOWLY CROSSES TO THE R. CHAISE LONGUE WHERE SHE STANDS HEROICALLY IN A STATE OF SHOCK) She's signed their charter, Nigel. What sort of a world have I brought you into ? This will kill your father.

MRS. MIDDY ENTERS D.L. AND RUSHES ACROSS TO LADY H. WHERE SHE FALLS ON HER KNEES BEFORE HER.

MRS. MIDDY   (DISTRAUGHT) Oh, my lady, is it true ? Are we all dismissed ? Please, my lady, I'm not like them, not in any way, not in the least. I appreciate your ladyship's kindness and generosity; I believe in the standards you're fighting to preserve. Please don't dismiss me ! I'll do anything: work in the kitchens, dig the garden, muck out the horses -

20

LADY H.   (PATTING HER HEAD) There, there, Mrs. Middy, of course I don't class you with those dreadful persons. I know how our great heritage is as precious to you as it is to myself.

MRS. MIDDY   (SIMPERING) Oh, my lady.

LADY H.   Of course you are not like them, my dear, but then your father was a gentleman, even if he was a grocer. (TO NIGEL. MOVING ROUND R. CHAISE LONGUE) You see, Nigel the difference breeding makes.

NIGEL   She's just sucking up to you, Mater. I'd rather have old Steward, at least he's not a creep.

LADY H.   (CLUTCHING HER BOSOM) Et tu, Brute !

MRS. MIDDY   I'm sure Master Nigel doesn't mean anything, your ladyship. Children can be so thoughtless, can't they ?

NIGEL   (JUMPING UP AND HURLING HIS MAGAZINE INTO THE FIREPLACE) I'm not a child ! And don't call me, 'Master' ! I'm Mister Nigel ! (STRIDING TO THE FRENCH WINDOW) I'm sorry, Mater, I can't see things your way anymore - I'm a man now and I must make my own decisions. I'm going to my workshop to dirty my hands ! (HE EXITS)

MRS. MIDDY PICKS UP THE MAGAZINE FROM THE FIREPLACE AND HOLDS IT THROUGH THE NEXT FEW LINES OF DIALOGUE

LADY H.   (SITTING) Oh dear, he can be so coarse. Naturally, it's from his father's side. (RECOVERING HER COMPOSURE) Now, Mrs. Middy, perhaps you could do me a little service ?

MRS. MIDDY   Anything, your ladyship.

LADY H.   Kindly tell that dreadful man, Stuart, that I'm willing to talk to him and then go to the stables and inform poor, dear Bond that he is required immediately.

MRS. MIDDY   Oh, m'lady, surely you are not going to give into that dreadful person's demands ?

LADY H.   Certainly not. I intend to humour him; play him as a cat does a mouse. I shall then reinstate Bond and order Stuart to leave. I would have liked Bond to have thrown him off the property but I fear he would not be up to it.

STEWARD ENTERS FROM U.R.

STEWARD   (MOVING TO L. OF LADY H.) You would, would yer ? Well, let me tell you, (SARCASTICALLY) your ladyship, that the days of the horsewhip have gone forever and the sooner you get that under your thick, aristocratic skull, the better.

MRS. M.   (ROLLING UP THE MAGAZINE AND ATTACKING HIM) How dare you speak to her ladyship like that ? You - you scum !

STEWARD   (STRUGGLING WITH HER) 'Scum' am I ? You fawning, little creep ! (HE PUSHES HER ONTO THE L. CHAISE LONGUE)

LADY H.   (RISING) Desist at once !

THEY STOP THEIR TUSSLE. STEWARD EASES U.R.

LADY H.   (SITTING) That's better. Millicent, my dear, do not degrade yourself; you cannot reason with his sort.

MRS. MIDDY   (RISING, FLUSTERED) Oh, my lady, you called me, you (CLASPING HER HANDS IN ECSTACY) called me - 'Millicent' !

LADY H.   Yes, my dear, such courage deserves reward. Now, run that little errand for me and leave me to deal with Stuart.

MRS. MIDDY   (PUTTING MAGAZINE ON COFFEE TABLE AND MOVING TOWARDS DOOR D. L.) Of course, your ladyship, I'll go at once.

LADY H.   And Millicent ?
MRS. MIDDY   (TURNING TO HER) Yes, m'lady ?
LADY H.   You may call me Cynthia.
MRS. MIDDY   (CURTSEYING) Oh, m'lady. (SIMPERING) Cynthia. (EXITS)
STEWARD   (MOVING DOWN BEHIND R. CH. LONGUE TO FIREPLACE)
    Reward ? You can call me Arthur 'till yer blue in the face; won't get
    yer nowhere.
LADY H.   I should never be guilty of such bad taste. Now, my man,
    say what you have to. I don't think you'll find me unreasonable.
STEWARD   (MOVING U.C. TO L. CHAIR IN RECESS) For a start my
    name's 'Steward' not 'Stewart', like you've been callin' me since I got
    here. From now on, you'll address me proper or we don't negotiate.
LADY H.   Very well, Mr. Steward, but what do you think you're doing,
    sitting in my presence.
STEWARD   Preparing to negotiate. Negotiations have to be made
    across a table, in a proper confronting position.
LADY H.   Oh, do they ? Well, I prefer to remain on my couch.
STEWARD   You either do things proper, according to the constitution,
    or it's all off, right ?
LADY H.   (RISING AND MOVING UP TO BELOW R. OF TABLE IN
    RECESS. CONDESCENDINGLY) Oh, very well, (SARCASTICALLY) Mr.
    Steward, if we must. (MOVING TO CHAIR INDICATED BY STEWARD)
    I can see what sort of an organisation your union is, Mr. Steward, by
    the way its chief official sits down before inviting a lady to sit.
STEWARD   You ain't no lady; you're management's representative and
    as such, on equal terms with the union's representative, that's me. We
    are negotiating as equals and there ain't no privilege for either side, see.

LADY H. TOSSES HER HEAD DISDAINFULLY AND SITS IN THE CHAIR
RIGHT. STEWARD CLEARS HIS THROAT AND DRAWS THE CHARTER
FROM HIS POCKET.

    The union has drawn up an agreement that sets out the minimum terms
    and conditions for the employment of our members. It is my duty to
    read out the aforesaid document in the presence of the employer.
LADY H.   (SNATCHING THE CHARTER) I haven't time, my man,
    to listen to all that claptrap. Let me see. (READS) "The Workers'
    Charter", good heavens, what next ? (READS) "Conditions of Employment:
    one, 'Hours of Work': no employee will work for more than sixty hours,
    calculated from Sunday to the following Saturday." Sixty hours ! What
    rubbish ! I expect that from my part-timers. What other absurdities have
    we got here ? (READS) "Holidays with Pay" ! Just as I thought, this is
    absolute anarchy ! (THROWING THE CHARTER AT HIM) I'm afraid
    you'll have to be realistic, my good man. These proposals are simply
    preposterous.
STEWARD   (LEANING OVER AND BEATING THE TABLE WITH HIS
    FIST) Preposterous are they ? Well, let me tell you, you'll think this a
    charter for bloody paradise compared with the next one !

LORD HARDCAST APPEARS IN THE DOORWAY U.R. WITH HIS SHOT-
GUN AT THE READY

LORD H.   Get yer hands up, you bounder ! Attack me wife, would ya,
    you sniffling, little cur !

STEWARD RISES, HOLDS UP HIS HANDS AND BACKS DOWN TO THE
DOOR D.L. HE STOPS WITH HIS BACK TO THE DOOR STARING AT
LORD H. WHO HAS MOVED DOWN TO D.R. KEEPING HIM COVERED

LADY H.   (RISING AND MOVING TO C.) Henry, you can't shoot him. It won't do any good.

LORD H.   Won't it, by jove, rotten, little bounder will be dead then, won't he ?

LADY H.   Henry, I've told you, you can't go around shooting the servants anymore.

LORD H.   Why not ? Deserted his post, didn't he ? Used to shoot the blighters for that during the war.

LADY H.   But we are not at war, Henry.

STEWARD   Don't be so sure, Hardcast. This means all-out war ! Harm me and you'll end up in jail. Times is different now; being a lord won't save you.

LORD H.   (ADVANCING SLOWLY ACROSS STAGE) Worth being locked away to pepper you, you scoundrel !

LADY H.   (PLACING HERSELF BETWEEN THEM) Henry, it would ruin us, we'd be socially de trop.

LORD H.   Still demned well worth it !

LADY H.   (DEFLECTING HIS GUN) But you'd be locked up, Henry.

LORD H.   (DODGING ROUND HER AND PINNING STEWARD TO THE DOOR) Worth it, to blast this little squirt !

LADY H.   (IN DESPERATION) But, you'll miss the cricket !

LORD H.   (SHOCKED) What's that ? Miss the cricket ! (STUNNED HE TOTTERS ACROSS R. TO COLLAPSE IN CHAIR D.R.) Yes, well, dash it all - not a violent man - rather talk - more civilised, what ? (SUPPORTING HIMSELF ON THE CHAIR) Miss the cricket, by gad, bit below the belt that. Feel a little faint. (HE COLLAPSES INTO CHAIR)

LADY H.   (AS HE DOES SO) Just collapse there, dear, and leave things to me as usual. (HER VOICE HARDENS) Now, Stuart, I've seen quite enough of your proposals and rather too much of you. I'm sorry to tell you - but we Hardcasts cannot be blackmailed.

LORD H.   (COMING TO) Hardcasts at Trafalgar, remember that.

LADY H.   Yes, dear. (TO STEWARD) So I suggest you get off our property before we set the hounds on you. You see, what you have overlooked in your dirty, little scheme is that people like us inspire in the lower orders a feeling of loyalty. Once you have gone, we shall be able to manage quite well with Mrs. Middy and dear, old Bond until the rest of the servants come to their senses.

LORD H.   (HALF RISING) Yes, by jove, they know which side their butter's breaded all right. (HE FALLS BACK INTO HIS CHAIR AGAIN)

STEWARD   (CROSSING TO LORD H. THREATENING HIM) I'm warning you, Hardcast, there'll be a hardening of attitudes and next time you won't find us willing to compromise.

BOND ENTERS U.L. HE LOOKS A BIT DISHEVELLED AND HAS A FEW WISPS OF HAY ABOUT HIS PERSON.

BOND   You wished to see me, m'lady ?

STEWARD RELEASES LORD H. AND TURNS TO STARE AT BOND

LADY H.   (TURNING AND SEEING BOND BUT SPEAKING TO STEWARD) If you wait one minute, Mr. Stuart, you'll see what real loyalty is.

STEWARD MOVES U.C. AS IF TO SPEAK TO BOND BUT LADY H. IS TOO QUICK FOR HIM AND TAKES BOND'S ARM

LADY H.   Ah, dear Bond, I've been so worried about you. (SHE LEADS HIM DOWN TO THE R. CHAISE LONGUE) Come and sit down, dear, old fellow.

BOND   (STARTLED) Sit, m'lady ?

LADY H.   (PUSHING HIM SO THAT HE COLLAPSES ONTO THE R. CHAISE LONGUE) But of course, just like old times. (MOVING D. AND ROUND THE R. CHAISE LONGUE FINISHING UP TALKING TO BOND ACROSS ITS BACK) Now, how have you been keeping ?

STEWARD EASES TO L. OF TABLE U. C.

BOND   Very well, m'lady, thank you.

LADY H.   Been warm enough at night, have you ?

BOND   Thank you, m'lady, yes. Groom has given me plenty of hay, keeps me very cosy, very cosy indeed.

LADY H.   Good. I'm so pleased. And Cook, has she been looking after you ?

BOND   Oh, yes, m'lady, she's given me my own dish - with 'Major' printed on it.

LORD H.   (TO HIMSELF) Dear old Major.

BOND   And today, m'lady, you'll never guess what.

LADY H.   (MOVING UP TO STEWARD. SMIRKING AT HIM) What, dear Bond ?

BOND   Mr. Steward paid me a great honour.

LADY H.   (TURNING SHARPLY TO HIM) Honour ? From Stuart ?

BOND   Yes, m'lady. (PUFFING OUT HIS CHEST) He's made me an honorary member of his union.

STEWARD NEATLY WHISKS THE L. CHAIR FROM THE TABLE U.C. TO BEHIND LADY H. WHO CLUTCHES HER BROW SPINS ROUND AND COLLAPSES INTO IT.

STEWARD   (WHIPPING THE 'CHARTER' OUT OF HIS POCKET AND THRUSTING IT OVER LADY H'S SHOULDER) Sign here !

CURTAIN

THE SAME MUCH LATER ON. WHEN THE CURTAIN RISES STEWARD IS ASLEEP ON THE R. CHAISE LONGUE AND DOLLY IS SITTING ON THE L. CHAISE LONGUE MANICURING HER NAILS. MRS. MIDDY ENTERS U.R. CARRYING A BUCKET AND MOP A COAL SCUTTLE AND A FEATHER DUSTER. SHE LOOKS DISDAINFULLY AT DOLLY AND THE SLEEPING STEWARD. THEN LEAVING THE MOP ETC. BY THE DOOR U.R. SHE FLOUNCES OUT D.L. WITH THE COAL SCUTTLE.

DOLLY   (CONTINUING TO MANICURE HER NAILS) I wish you hadn't got us two and a half hours for dinner break, Mr. Steward. The time don't half go slowly. (SHE LOOKS UP BUT IS ONLY ANSWERED BY A SNORE FROM STEWARD.)

MRS. MIDDY ENTERS D.L. WITHOUT THE COAL SCUTTLE GOES UP TO THE FRENCH WINDOW AND BEGINS TO DUST.

MRS. MIDDY   The top of this window is disgusting; it looks as if it hasn't been touched for months.
DOLLY   I don't suppose it has.
MRS. MIDDY   How you can sit there, my girl, calmly fiddling with your nails and say that, I don't know, when the cleaning of this room is your responsibility.
DOLLY   Can't dust anything above five feet can I ? Against union regulations. Safety, ain't it ? Might strain me arm muscles.
MRS. MIDDY   I'd like to strain your neck. If you're not allowed to do it, who's going to ?
DOLLY   Dunno, you or her, I suppose.
MRS. MIDDY   (SHOCKED) Her ? You mean her ladyship ?
DOLLY   Well, you and her are the only ones who ain't in the union.
MRS. MIDDY   Union ! I'm sick of hearing about this wretched union.
DOLLY   You want to join so as she can't put upon yer.
MRS. MIDDY   Join, I'd rather die !
DOLLY   Suit yerself.
MRS. MIDDY   (PUTTING DOWN HER FEATHER DUSTER AND PICKING UP THE BUCKET AND MOP) I'll just have to get the steps and do these windows properly.(SHE MOVES TO THE DOOR D.L. AND TURNS TO DOLLY) You wait, my girl, one of these days her ladyship will get the better of this precious union of yours. Then we'll see. She'll not forget those who stuck by her.
DOLLY   Shouldn't bank on it, if I was you.
MRS. MIDDY   But you are not me; you are nothing like me; for which I I thank God ! (SHE EXITS)

DOLLY SHRUGS HER SHOULDERS AND GOES ON MANICURING HER NAILS. LORD H. ENTERS U.R. AND TIPTOES DOWN TO DOLLY'S R. KEEPING HIS EYES ON THE SLEEPING STEWARD AS HE DOES SO.

LORD H.   (IN A STAGE WHISPER) I say, frightfully sorry to interrupt your lunch break and all that. Don't happen to have seen Mrs. Middy, I suppose. Need her to wait at lunch. Never about when one wants her. You know how it is.
DOLLY   Gone to get the steps to do the winder. I'll tell her if you like. (INDICATING STEWARD) If he don't wake up that is. I'm not supposed to pass messages; not in my job specification.
LORD H.   No, no, quite understand. Musn't upset Steward. Don't want you all out again, what ?

THE PHONE RINGS. LORD H. LOOKS AGHAST TERRIFIED THAT IT
WILL WAKE STEWARD. HE CHARGES ACROSS L. AND SNATCHES UP
THE RECEIVER

LORD H.   (INTO THE PHONE) I thought I made it plain there were
to be no calls from eleven thirty 'till two. Well, it's dashed bad form.
The drawing room is out of bounds for the family during the servants'
lunch break. What ? No, I can't ! Go away !

STEWARD WAKES UP AND LOOKS AROUND SLEEPILY

Now look what you've done ! (SLAMMING DOWN THE RECEIVER AND
CROSSING INGRATIATINGLY TO STEWARD'S L.) Frightfully sorry, old
boy, that was that silly old fool, Sir Perigrine. Not up with the times,
don't ya know; non compos mentis; tempus fugit, what ?
STEWARD   You what ?
LORD H.   Old boy's a bit past it; don't know times have changed.
STEWARD   He'll have to learn then, won't he ?
LORD H.   Not really a friend of mine, ya know: too much old guard,
- er, rather square, what ?
STEWARD   (LOOKING AT HIS WATCH) Here, not two o'clock is it ?
LORD H.   (CROSSING ABOVE R. CHAISE LONGUE TO EXIT U.R.
BUT STOPPING AS A THOUGHT STRIKES HIM) No, no, 'course not,
awfully bad form. (COMING BACK BEHIND R. CHAISE LONGUE) I say,
old boy, as I am here, would you mind frightfully if I ask a bit of a
favour ?
STEWARD   Negotiations must be conducted on a formal basis within
properly convened meetings. As the representative of the union I am not
empowered to make ad hoc arrangements.
LORD H.   (MOVING AROUND CHAISE LONGUE TO STEWARD'S L.)
No, well one wouldn't expect it, would one. Actually, this little favour
falls within the properly constituted agreement - I think.
STEWARD   Oh yus, found a loophole, have yer ?
LORD H.   Good heavens, no; nothing underhand I assure you. It's just
that I'd like the Rolls tomorrow instead of Thursday. That's all right,
ain't it ? I mean it does say one day a week.
STEWARD   And it don't specify which day ?
LORD H.   No.
STEWARD   We'll have to sort that out then.
DOLLY   You can't have it anyhow, 'cause Homage has taken it.
Took his kids to the sea, ain't he. Won't be back 'till Friday.
LORD H.   Well, dash it all, not quite playing the game is it ?
STEWARD   Free use of car was part of the agreement, wan't it ?
LORD H.   Yes, but -
STEWARD   Trying to renegue now, are we ? Absolutely typical !
LORD H.   No, no, it doesn't matter. I can easily hire a car from the
village. Nigel will drive.
STEWARD   Got a union card then, has he ?
LORD H.   Don't think so, no.
STEWARD   Can't take yer then, can he ? Not unless he wants ter be
the cause of industrial action.
LORD H.   I say, that's a bit thick.
STEWARD   Thin end of the wedge, mate. We start lettin' people drive
themselves around and where will our chauffeurs be ? Hadn't thought of
that, had yer ?
LORD H.   Well, no, hadn't actually occurred to me. Not frightfully
up in this sort of thing, I suppose.

STEWARD   You'll catch on, mate, don't you worry.

THE SOUND OF THE HUNT IS HEARD IN THE DISTANCE

LORD H.   Good Lord, nobody told me they were hunting today !
(RUSHING TO THE WINDOW U. L. AS THE SOUND INCREASES AND
STARING OUT AS THE HUNT PASSES AND FADES AWAY INTO THE
DISTANCE) Jumping jodhpurs ! That was Serf, riding my Empress !

STEWARD   You should read the small print, mate. Free use of the
horses is part of his perks.

LORD H.   Great gadflies, did I sign that ?

LADY H. ENTERS U.R. AND CROSSES TO C.

LADY H.   Are we never going to have lunch, Henry ? If it gets any
later, we'll be having it with afternoon tea. (CALLING) Millicent !

LORD H.   (BREAKING DOWN R. WITH HIS FINGER TO HIS LIPS)
Shush, dear ! It's not two o'clock yet.

LORD H. TIPTOES TO THE FIREPLACE AS MRS. MIDDY ENTERS D.L.

MRS MIDDY   Yes, Cynthia ?

LADY H.   Ah, Millicent dear, you'll have to come and wait on table.

MRS. MIDDY Wait at table, Cynthia ? But I've already cooked lunch,
seen to the laundry, pruned the roses and mended the fence. Now you
want me to serve lunch just as I was getting the steps to dust this
window.

LADY H.   Well, it can't be helped, dear. You know that awful Stuart
won't start until two.

MRS. MIDDY Oh, very well, Cynthia, just for you, dear. (SHE TURNS
TO EXIT D.L.) I'll borrow one of the maids' caps.

STEWARD   Oh no you won't ! That's encroaching on my members'
work, that is. (TURNING TO LORD H.) You let her serve at table and
you've got a demarcation dispute on yer hands, Hardcast, you have.

LORD H.   But, dash it, none of you union people will do it until two
o'clock !

STEWARD   That's when lunch will have to be then, ain't it.

LADY H.   Very well, my good man, drastic illnesses demand drastic
cures: Lord Hardcast and I will serve ourselves with lunch. Unless that
contravenes one of your precious regulations.

STEWARD   (TAKING A PENCIL FROM BEHIND HIS EAR AND A
SMALL NOTEBOOK FROM HIS POCKET) Not yet it don't. (HE LICKS THE
PENCIL AND MAKES A NOTE IN HIS BOOK)

LADY H.   Come, Henry !

STEWARD   I'll make a note of it though.

LADY H.   Come, Millicent, this room is distinctly overcrowded !

MRS. MIDDY MOVES TO EXIT U.R.

Never mind about the caps, dear, (FOLLOWING HER) you can show us
how it's done. (TURNING AT THE EXIT) Come, Henry !

LORD H.   (CROSSING TO C. AND TURNING TO STEWARD. VERY
APOLOGETIC) Have to go, old boy. Promised to go fishing with dear,
old Bond.

HE CREEPS UP TO EXIT U.L. BUT IS STOPPED BY LADY H'S IMPERIOUS
VOICE.

LADY H.   Stop apologising to the lower orders, Henry and come
along at once !

LORD H. TURNS AND MEEKLY FOLLOWS LADY H.

STEWARD   At the double !

LORD H. LEAPS INTO THE AIR BEFORE EXITING

(RISING AND STRETCHING) Reckon I need some fresh air after that lot. Think I'll go for a little stroll, girl, before we start back. Let me dinner go down so I'm ready for tea break this arternoon.

DOLLY   Nothin' but bloomin' breaks; get right fed up. Reckon breaks are bloomin' boring. What yer keep makin' them longer for ?

STEWARD   Got to negotiate something, girl. We've got a twenty hour week, two months holiday with pay, retirement at forty. Gettin' ruddy difficult to think up new demands, I can tell yer. We've gottem on the run though, you mark my words. Just give me time and we'll evict the lot of 'em. Serve the old devils right.

DOLLY   Evict them ? That's going a bit far, ain't it ? I mean, it is their house.

STEWARD   Oh yes, by law, maybe it is.   But how did they get it, eh ? Ask yerself that. By the sweat of our brows, that's how.

DOLLY   Well, you ain't done a lot of sweatin' lately that I can see.

STEWARD   Watch it, girl, or you'll be losing your union card ! Right, I'm off. (HE MOVES U.L. TO EXIT) And just watch you don't lift a finger 'till it strikes two o'clock. (HE EXITS)

NIGEL ENTERS U.R.

NIGEL   (COMING DOWN C.) Do you mind if I come in, Miss Dolly?

DOLLY   It's all right, don't look so nervous. He's gone for a walk. Won't see him again 'till afternoon tea break.

NIGEL   Sure you don't mind ?

DOLLY   What ?

NIGEL   Me, interrupting your lunch hour ?

DOLLY   Two and a half hours.

NIGEL   Yes, well, I was speaking figuratively.

DOLLY   Were you now ?

NIGEL   Yes. (INDICATING THE R. CHAISE LONGUE) May I sit down ?

DOLLY   Suit yerself; your house.

NIGEL   Oh, is it ? But still the thing to ask a lady's permission, what ?

DOLLY   Ooh, 'Lady', that's nice.

NIGEL FIDDLES UNCOMFORTABLY WITH HIS TIE

DOLLY
NIGEL   (TOGETHER) Penny for them ?

THEY BOTH LAUGH

DOLLY   You must be a thought-reader.

NIGEL   Wish I were. Like to know what you're thinking, Dolly.

DOLLY   Might give yer a bit of a shock. Tell me what you're thinking first and I might let on.

NIGEL   I'm thinking - that I'm thinking of you everyday; that you're an absolutely first-rate sort of gel and that I'm pretty certain I've fallen in love with you. There, your turn.

DOLLY   Well, knock me down wiv a feather, fancy you taking a shine to a little Miss Nobody like me.

NIGEL   Stop fooling and come over here.

28

DOLLY   (CLOWNING) Ooh, Mr. Nigel, sir, how do I know your
    intentions are honourable ? How do I know you won't take advantage of
    a poor girl like me ?
NIGEL   Please be serious, Dolly and come and sit here.
DOLLY   (RISING AND CROSSING U.R. TO GO ROUND THE R.
    CHAISE LONGUE) Oh, but I am serious, Mister Nigel, and so was my
    mum when she said you gentlemen has only one interest in poor girls
    like me. (SHE SITS BELOW HIM ON THE R. CHAISE LONGUE)
NIGEL   That's never been true of me, Dolly; you know that.
    Anyway all that class stuff is absolute tosh now. Will you marry me ?
DOLLY   Marry you ? And what about your mother ?
NIGEL   I don't care anymore what mother says or thinks. It's you
    I want, Dolly, you and only you.
DOLLY   Marry me. It will kill her.
NIGEL   Oh, no it won't. Mother's a survivor; the day of judgement
    holds no fear for her. Anyway, it's time she forgot all this class
    claptrap and realised that we are all equal.
DOLLY   You try telling that to old Steward. He thinks nobody's
    equal to him. And her ladyship won't change neither. She'd go bananas
    if she could see us now.
NIGEL   I'll make her see, Dolly, and if she won't, well, she'll just
    have to live with it, that's all.
DOLLY   That's all you know.
NIGEL   All I know, Dolly, is that I love you and will never be
    happy again unless you marry me. Will you, Dolly ? Put a chap out of
    his misery and say you will.
DOLLY   I don't know, Nigel. It won't half cause a lot of trouble.
NIGEL   But you do want to, don't you, Dolly ?
DOLLY   All right then; let 'em lump it if they don't like it. That's
    what I says.
NIGEL   The world can go hang !
DOLLY   Hang the bloody world !

THEY KISS

LADY H.   (OFF) Oh, and then, Millicent dear, you can polish the
    silver. Only don't dally, dear, or you'll be late to see to the horses.

NIGEL AND DOLLY SPRING APART ON HEARING HER VOICE AND
JUMP TO THEIR FEET

DOLLY   Quick, Nigel, we musn't let on yet. Let's wait a bit,
    please !
NIGEL   All right, my sweet, sweet Dolly. Trust your Nigel. (GOING
    TO THE EXIT U.L.) I'll be in my workshop if you want me. Bye for
    now, darling. (HE EXITS)

DOLLY BLOWS HIM A KISS AS HE GOES. LADY H. ENTERS

LADY H.   Was that Nigel, Dolly ?
DOLLY   Nigel, m'lady ?
LADY H.   I thought I heard his voice. I never see him these days;
    always in that ghastly workshop of his. Never mind, it was you I wanted
    to see.
DOLLY   Me, m'lady ?
LADY H.   (MOVING TO SIT ON THE R. CHAISE LONGUE) Come and
    sit down, dear. I'd like a chat with you.
DOLLY   Sit, m'lady ?

LADY H.   Nothing odd about that, dear, is there ?

DOLLY   Not if you say so, m'lady. (SHE SITS HESITATINGLY BELOW LADY H. ON THE CHAISE LONGUE)

LADY H.   Of course not. Now, dear, - it's very difficult - we of the quality are not very good at showing our feelings. I was always brought up to believe that displaying emotion is a continental weakness and simply not done in England. I have not changed from this belief of course but I sometimes feel that because of our breeding, our natural reticence, we are often misunderstood by the lower orders and it has occurred to me, Dolly, that you might not realise just how much we admire and value you.

DOLLY   Me, your ladyship ?

LADY H.   Yes, dear. Oh, I know I've sometimes appeared hard, even inconsiderate but that was all part of your training and had to be done no matter how painful to me personally at the time.

DOLLY   Well, I never.

LADY H.   Duty before sentiment, that's the family motto, you know. But I have been worried about you lately, Dolly.

DOLLY   Worried, m'lady ? About me ?

LADY H.   Yes, I feel you are too much under the influence of that vulgar man, Stuart. I fear he's abusing you, my dear.

DOLLY   Oh no, your ladyship, he's never laid a finger on me.

LADY H.   Not in that way, dear. I meant robbing you of your independence. Tell me, do you really like these long lunch breaks ?

DOLLY   No, I don't. I was tellin' him just now, I think they're bloomin' boring . Oh, beggin' your ladyship's pardon.

LADY H.   Not at all, my dear. It was just as I thought. You see men like Stuart can't bear their underlings to have a shred of personal freedom. You don't want to be robbed of your right to choose, do you, Dolly ?

DOLLY   No, m'lady, 'course not. (PAUSE) M'lady ?

LADY H.   Yes, Dolly ?

DOLLY   Did I have that before ? Before Mr. Steward come, I mean.

LADY H.   It would only have been a matter of time, my dear but just as we felt you were mature enough to make your own decisions, along comes this hateful man, Stuart, and ruins everything for all of us.

DOLLY   Well I don't know. I mean he has made things better for us in some ways. I mean, I get more money in a week now than I did in a year and I can go and see me old mum anytime I like.

LADY H.   Just a sprat to catch a mackerel, dear, I'm afraid. Once he has complete power and we're not here to protect your interests, he'll take away all those benefits that you think you've been given. I'm sure you must see that, dear. I've had a word with Cook and she's now of my opinion: "had a real eye-opener", to use her quaint expression.

DOLLY   Well, of course, if Mrs. Pottage thinks -

LADY H.   She does, dear, she does.

DOLLY   P'raps you're right then.

LADY H.   I am, dear, most assuredly, mark my words. (RISING) Now, I musn't delay you any more or you'll miss your working time, won't you. I want to have a chat with Doris and Margaret. I'm so glad, dear, that we understand each other so well.

LADY H. EXITS U.R. AS MRS. MIDDY ENTERS U.R. CARRYING THE STEPS

LADY H.   There you are, Millicent. Carry on with the dusting.(EXITS)
MRS. MIDDY   It's gone two, so would it be in order for me to ask for a little help with the dusting ?
DOLLY   (MOVING UP TO HER) I'll take the steps shall I ?
MRS. MIDDY   (SARCASTICALLY) If you're sure it's not against the union's regulations to carry such heavy things.
DOLLY   Maybe it is and maybe it ain't.   I'm fed up with his stupid regulations. (SHE TAKES THE STEPS FROM MRS. MIDDY)

STEWARD ENTERS U.L.

STEWARD   Hello, hello and what are you up to then ?
DOLLY   Startin' work. It's gone two.
STEWARD   (POINTING AT THE STEPS) You're not carrying them on yer own, girl. Reckon they must weigh all of ten pounds. Just a minute. (HE TAKES OUT A RULE BOOK AND CONSULTS IT) Ten pounds ? Ah, just as I thought: it'll need three of you.
MRS. MIDDY   What rubbish. I carried them in myself not more than two minutes ago.
STEWARD   Did you now ? But then you ain't in the union.
MRS. MIDDY   No, thank God !
STEWARD   (TO DOLLY) Mark what I say, girl. You get two of the others to help you now !

DOLLY PUTS THE STEPS DOWN IN THE ARCHWAY U.R. TOSSES HER HEAD AT STEWARD AND EXITS U.R.

MRS. MIDDY   Really, Mr. Steward, you're making life quite impossible for her ladyship, not to mention myself.
STEWARD   Am I now ?
MRS. MIDDY   Yes, I sometimes think you do it to humiliate us both.
STEWARD   Do you now ?
MRS. MIDDY   A sort of revenge for the past. No good will come of it you know. If you go on bleeding her ladyship; demanding higher and higher wages, she'll be forced to move to the lodge and where will we be then ?
STEWARD   She tell you that, did she ? She's stringing you along.
MRS. MIDDY   Her ladyship and I are very close. She may string you along, as you put it, Mr. Steward but Cynthia would never deliberately mislead me.
STEWARD   No ?
MRS. MIDDY   (MOVING DOWN TO THE EXIT D.L.) No, emphatically, no.
STEWARD   (CALLING AFTER HER) You look tired to me.
MRS. MIDDY   (STOPPING IN HER TRACKS AND TURNING TO HIM) What ?
STEWARD   Worn out before your time.
MRS. MIDDY   (PUTTING HER HAND TO HER HEAD) Yes, I do feel - Mr. Steward, a gentleman never tells a lady that she looks tired or calls her old.
STEWARD   (MOVING ABOVE L. CHAISE LONGUE TO MRS. M.) No, but then I ain't no gentleman. A gentleman Mrs. Middy, wouldn't even notice how his servants might look. In the union it's different: we're concerned about all our members. (HE TAKES HER ARM AND GUIDES HER ACROSS TO THE R. CHAISE LONGUE) Now, you come and sit down and have a little rest.
MRS. MIDDY (SITTING ON D.S. END) Sit down, how lovely. (RISING) No, I can't: there's so much to do. I promised her ladyship I'd polish the silver, muck out the horses, mend the broken gutter. Oh dear, oh dear-

STEWARD   (FORCING HER TO SIT) You sit down and take it easy.
MRS. MIDDY   Well, perhaps for one minute.

STEWARD ARRANGES THE CUSHIONS FOR HER

You're very kind, Mr. Steward, I never knew. I'm afraid
I've rather misjudged you. Her ladyship has always said -
STEWARD   Well she would, wouldn't she. She can't bear anyone who
stands up to her.
MRS. MIDDY   It's true she has a very strong character.
STEWARD   Strong character, be blowed ! She's a vindictive old -
MRS. MIDDY   (PUTTING HER HANDS OVER HER EARS) Mr. Steward,
you are speaking of a dear friend of mine !
STEWARD   Friend ? Some friend ! She treats you like a drudge.
MRS. MIDDY   It's true she can be very demanding but then she has a
great position and tradition to uphold.
STEWARD   Position, tradition ? My arse !
MRS. MIDDY   Mr. Steward !
STEWARD   (SITTING BESIDE HER) She's not going to give up any of
her perks, that's all that means. I tell you, Mrs. Middy, there's only one
way you'll get the old blood-sucker off your back and that's by joining
the union.

DOLLY ENTERS U.R. SHE PICKS UP THE STEPS, PULLS A FACE AT
STEWARD AND CARRIES THEM UP TO THE WINDOW U.L. WHERE SHE
BEGINS DUSTING WITH THE FEATHER DUSTER.

MRS. MIDDY   Join the union. Oh, no, I couldn't do that, Mr. Steward.
It would upset dear Cynthia so.

LADY H. ENTERS U.R.

STEWARD   Upset dear Cynthia, I'd bloody well like to - !
LADY H.   Millicent, what are you doing with that - that man ?
MRS. MIDDY   (LEAPING TO HER FEET) Nothing, dear, we were just
talking. Actually, Mr. Steward was being very kind.
LADY H.   Kind ? That man ? You were fraternising. He was trying
to talk you into joining his wretched union.
MRS. MIDDY   Oh, but I wouldn't, dear, I wouldn't . I could never betray
you, Cynthia dear; you know that.

STEWARD SPOTS DOLLY ON THE STEPS DUSTING THE CURTAINS. HE
MOVES QUICKLY TO HER R.

STEWARD   Dolly, what the 'ell do you think you're doing, girl !
You're contravening safety regulations !
DOLLY   (FLICKING HIM WITH THE FEATHER DUSTER) Flip to
your old regulations ! Can't do this, can't do that. You'll be tellin' me
when I can sneeze next !
LADY H.   (TO DOLLY) That's the spirit, my girl. Show him you have
a mind of your own ! Eh, Millicent ?
STEWARD   (TO LADY H.) This is your doing, you interfering old
crone ! I know what you've been up to: undermining the authority of the
union !
MRS. MIDDY   How dare you speak to her ladyship like that, you, you -
heathen !
LADY H.   It's all right, Millicent, leave this to me. (TO STEWARD)
Now, you listen to me, my good man. My staff are getting fed up with
your precious union. You've had a good run for your money but the
game is up. Cook is ready to resign and the others are thinking about it.
I'm afraid your day is almost over.

32

STEWARD   Over is it ! We haven't got started yet so you listen to me ! From tomorrow, I'm instituting a closed shop.

LADY H.   A closed shop ?

STEWARD   Yes, either you join the union or you don't work. (TO MRS. MIDDY) So you can stick that up your jumper ! (TO DOLLY) And as for them what don't obey union rules, they'll lose their cards and then they won't work neither.

LADY H.   You can't do this ! It's outrageous !

STEWARD   (MARCHING TO THE DOOR D.L.) I'm doing it !

LADY H.   Then democracy and freedom are dead.

STEWARD   (TURNING TO HER) And so is bloody tyranny ! (MAKING A RUDE GESTURE TO HER THEN MARCHING OFF L.) Up the union and up yours !

LADY H.   (COLLAPSING ON THE R. CHAISE LONGUE) Oh dear, I feel quite faint. It's the end of the fight, Millicent. A great tradition, Nigel's heritage, gone for ever.

MRS. MIDDY   Something will turn up, dear, you'll see.

LADY H.   (STARING INTO SPACE) No dear, we must accept change; adapt or perish.

NIGEL ENTERS U.L. TAKES DOLLY'S HAND AND HELPS HER DOWN FROM THE STEPS

DOLLY   Not now, for heavens sake, Nigel. It's not the time !

NIGEL   Yes, Dolly, there'll never be a better. Come on ! (HE COMES DOWN TO LADY H'S L. BRINGING DOLLY WITH HIM) Mother, I have something to tell you. I know it will come as a great shock but the fact is - Dolly and I are going to get married.

LADY H.   (SITTING BOLT UPRIGHT) You and Dolly ? (RISING) You and Dolly, marry ?

NIGEL   Yes, Mother, I'm sorry but my mind's made up.

LADY H.   (RAISING HER HANDS AS IF IN HORROR) I can't believe it ! That I should bear a son, a Hardcast, who is now - to marry into the union ! (TAKING THEIR HANDS) Bless you, my children !

CURTAIN

ACT II Sc.2.

THE SAME LATER ON STILL. WHEN THE CURTAIN RISES LADY H. IS STANDING ON TOP OF THE STEPS U.C. SHE IS DUSTING THE FRENCH WINDOW. LORD H. IS KNEELING BEHIND THE R. CHAISE LONGUE. HE IS USING A BRUSH AND PAN TO BRUSH THE CARPET BUT HAS THE BRUSH UPSIDE DOWN. HE AND LADY H. ARE WEARING APRONS. DOLLY ENTERS R. CARRYING A COAL SCUTTLE WHICH SHE PLACES IN FRONT OF THE EMPTY FIREPLACE. HER DRESS REMAINS THE SAME EXCEPT THAT NOW SHE WEARING SOME EXPENSIVE JEWELLERY.

LADY H.   I knew that man, Stuart, was not to be trusted. It's absolutely disgraceful, expelling poor Dolly from the union just because she married Nigel.

LORD H'S HEAD APPEARS OVER THE TOP OF THE CHAISE LONGUE

LORD H.   The man's an out-and-out blackguard, a scoundrel of the the first order ! No moral standards left these days that's the trouble. (HIS HEAD DISAPPEARS)

LADY H.   I blame the comprehensives.

33

LORD H.   (RAISING HIS HEAD ABOVE THE CHAISE LONGUE) Thank
    God they left us Eton. (HIS HEAD DISAPPEARS)
DOLLY   It doesn't matter, it really doesn't. At least Nigel and me
    can do what we like with our time off. Like the good, old days, ain't it
    now ?
LADY H.   What are you talking about, Dolly ? It's not a bit like the
    good, old days, not in any way.
DOLLY   Maybe it ain't for you.
LADY H.   You're a Hardcast now, my girl - something I would not
    have wished of course but there we are - and as such you must learn to
    stand aloof and look down on the world.(SHE NEARLY LOSES HER
    BALANCE) It's difficult, I know, to keep one's position in these days but
    as a Hardcast you must learn. The days when you were a little domestic
    are over.
LORD H.   (HIS HEAD APPEARING AGAIN) The Hardcasts were at
    Waterloo, you know. (HIS HEAD DISAPPEARS AGAIN)
DOLLY   Waterloo, fancy that. I have come up in the world. Now,
    I not only do all the work I did before but most of Steward's as well.
LADY H.   (DESCENDING FROM THE STEPS) How you can complain
    when you see what Lord Henry and myself have suffered, is beyond me.

LORD H. CRAWLS ROUND THE U.S. END OF THE CHAISE LONGUE. HE
IS ATTEMPTING TO BRUSH THE CARPET BUT HAS THE BRUSH UPSIDE
DOWN.

LADY H.   Henry, I'm sure that brush works the other way up, dear.

LADY H. DESCENDS THE STEPS. DOLLY LAUGHS AT LORD H.

LADY H.   Nothing to laugh at, Dolly.
LORD H.   (TURNING THE BRUSH OVER) Demned, cock-eyed world:
    manes should be uppermost ! (HE BRUSHES HIS WAY ACROSS TO
    LADY H.)
DOLLY   Well, I'm the Honourable Mrs. Hardcast whether you like
    it or not. And talking of things to learn, I reckon you need a bit of
    help from me, not the other way round.
LADY H.   Yes, you're right, dear, of course. I'm sorry. It's just so
    hard to adapt. (SHE LIFTS HER LEGS TO ALLOW LORD H. TO SWEEP
    UNDER THEM) So disappointing; I expected so much from this marriage.
DOLLY   Did you now ? Not your son's happiness, that's for sure.
    You thought you'd be able to get old Steward out once you'd got your
    foot in the door and take over the union so that you could have us all
    kowtowing to yer, like in the old days.

LORD H. STARES AT DOLLY AS HE SCRAMBLES TO HIS FEET

LADY H.   (PRETENDING TO SOB) How could you, Dolly, how could
    you ?
LORD H.   (TO LADY H.) I say, steady on, old gel !

LORD H. LOOKS DESPERATELY FROM LADY H. TO DOLLY AND BACK
AGAIN. THEN IN HIS CONFUSION HE EMPTIES HIS DUSTPAN INTO HIS
APRON POCKET AND RUSHES U.L. TO HURL THE DUSTPAN INTO THE
GARDEN.
DOLLY   (SITTING ON THE R. CHAISE LONGUE) I'm sorry, I
    should not have said that. Not our usual selves are we ? But we shall
    all have to get used to the fact that I ain't no longer in the union.

LADY H.   (RECOVERING) We must stick together, whatever happens, we must stick together; that's all that matters. (WIPING HER EYES) To think that that creature, Stuart, could reduce me to this. Henry, do you know, I've shed a real tear.

LORD H.   (COMING SLOWLY DOWN TO HER) Have you, my dear ? (INSPECTING) Good Lord, so you have. (SITTING BESIDE HER) Good job you're not a fellah, what ?

LADY H.   It's so hard to accept that things have changed and there's simply nothing one can do about it. (PAUSE) And what time do we expect the staff back from these ghastly dog races, Dolly ?

DOLLY   Old Steward usually gets back from them about ten. Just depends on whether they stay drinking or not.

LADY H.   How Mrs. Middy could bring herself to - I mean, Stuart and the others, yes, I can see them liking such low entertainment but I would have thought -

DOLLY   She don't have a lot of option now she's in the union, does she ?

LADY H.   I suppose not but the woman's quite refined in a coarse sort of way.

DOLLY   (JUMPING UP) I think what we all need is a drink.

LADY H.   That would be lovely but I expect Stuart's locked the drinks cabinet.

DOLLY   Don't matter. I know where he hides the key. Shall I get us all one, on a tray like old times ?

LADY H.   (RISING AND FORCING HER GENTLY TO SIT) No, dear, I shall wait on you, just to make amends. (TO LORD H.) What would you like, Henry, a port or a whisky ?

LORD H.   Gad, can't remember the difference now, me dear. Try anything liquid.

LADY H.   What for you, Dolly dear ?

DOLLY   Gin and something then, Mum.

LADY H.   (WINCING) "Gin and something then, Mum" ! (SHE MOVES DOWN TO THE DOOR D.L. AND TURNS BACK TO DOLLY) Now, where shall I find the key ?

DOLLY   It's in that suit of armour in the 'all: in the 'and, it comes off.

LADY H.   " In the 'and; it comes off". The left hand, of course ?

DOLLY   Yes.

LADY H.   Just as I expected. (SHE EXITS)

LORD H.   Musn't mind Cynthia, me dear, means well ya know; little hard-mouthed that's all. Don't respond to the bit too well. She's a great jumper though; no fence puts her orf.

DOLLY   It's all right, - Dad. I know it's not easy for either of you when you've been used to so much. I didn't have much to lose, did I ?

LORD H.   Still hard on the hoof, becoming a Hardcast these days. Ever tell you there were Hardcasts at Agincourt ?

DOLLY   (SMILING) I think so.

LORD H.   Waterloo ?

DOLLY NODS

LORD H.   Trafalgar ?

DOLLY NODS AGAIN

LORD H.   Thought I had. (PAUSE) Miss the hunting ya know. Like to to see you on a horse; got the seat for it.

DOLLY   Doesn't matter, Dad. Forget about it.

LORD H.   Make the best of things, what ? You're a real Hardcast, me dear, proud of ya.

NIGEL ENTERS U.L. AND MOVES TO C. HE IS WEARING A WHITE COAT

Hello, me boy, not going to do a spot of umpiring are you ?

NIGEL   No, Father, it's my workshop coat.

DOLLY   (RISING AND MOVING D.R.) He's a scientist these days, aren't you, darling ?

NIGEL   It works, Dolly, it actually works !

LORD H.   What does, me boy, another demned, mechanical gadget, I'll be bound.

NIGEL   No, Dad, I'm into electronics these days.

LORD H.   Electronics ? Politics are no good now, me boy: too many demned, free votes these days.

NIGEL   Nothing to do with elections, father. Simple electronical control, data storage, computation and all that.

LORD H.   Beyond me, me boy. Can't teach an old dog new tricks, eh what ?

LADY H.   (ENTERING D.L.) Ah, Nigel, how nice to see you.

DOLLY   He's finished his project, Mum, and it works.

LADY H.   How nice - "Mum". I've done the drinks but I need a tray.

DOLLY   In the cupboard, next to the pantry, where they've always been kept.

LADY H.   (GOING BACK TO THE DOOR D.L.) Of course, dear. I wondered what that door was for.

NIGEL   (MOVING TO HER) No, wait a moment, Mother. Let me get the drinks for you.

LADY H.   (STAGGERING ACROSS TO SIT ON THE R. CHAISE LONGUE) Well, if you insist, dear. I do feel a little exhausted from pouring them.

NIGEL EXITS D.L.

LORD H.   Need a bit of exercise in the paddock, me dear, if you ask me.

LADY H.   Henry, I wish you wouldn't keep confusing me with your mare.

LORD H.   Fine animal, Empress, almost human.

LADY H.   What a wonderful courtier you would have made, Henry.

LORD H.   Courtier, eh, m'dear ? There were Hardcasts at Hampton.

NIGEL ENTERS D.L. CARRYING A CONTROL UNIT LIKE THOSE USED TO CONTROL MODEL AIRCRAFT

LADY H.   Yes, dear.

NIGEL   (MOVING TO U.C.) Are we all ready ? Ring the bell for drinks, Dolly.

LADY H.   Ring ?

NIGEL   Yes.

DOLLY RINGS THE BELL

LADY H.   I say what fun ! Quite like old times.

NIGEL OPERATES THE CONTROLS AND AT THE SAME TIME HOLDS OPEN THE DOOR D.L. CHIPPY ENTERS CARRYING THE DRINKS.

LADY H.   (RISING AND SCREAMING) Aa-ah !
LORD H.   Suffering stirrups ! (HE DIVES BEHIND THE L. CHAISE L.)

CHIPPY CROSSES WITH THE TRAY OF DRINKS TO LADY H.

               (LOOKING OVER THE BACK OF THE CHAISE LONGUE)
   What on earth's that , me boy ?
NIGEL   It's all right, nothing to be alarmed about. Just watch.

CHIPPY MOVES UNSTEADILY FROM ONE TO THE OTHER SERVING THE
DRINKS IN A CLUMSY MECHANICAL FASHION. HE ENDS UP WITH
LORD H. WHO SNATCHES IT AND DOWNS IT IN ONE GULP BEFORE
SITTING ON THE CHAISE LONGUE.

LADY H.   Well, I'm sure it's very nice, dear, and a lot of fun but
   not very practical is it ? I mean you can hardly trust it with the bone
   china.
LORD H.   Can't catch rabbits, can it ?
NIGEL   Not yet but this is only a beginning. (TAKING THE TRAY
   FROM CHIPPY AND PLACING IT ON THE TABLE U.C.) The next
   model will be better, you'll see.
LORD H.   Don't respond to the whip, do it ?
NIGEL   'Fraid not, Father, but I have programmed it for other
   things, only I can't remember what they are. Let's try a code at random,
   shall we ?

NIGEL PRESSES A SEQUENCE OF BUTTONS. CHIPPY SPINS ROUND
WILDLY MOVES A FEW PACES TURNS AND THEN CONTINUES TO
LADY H. WHERE HE PROCEEDS TO PLUCK AT HER DRESS

LADY H.   (TRYING TO BEAT CHIPPY OFF) Nigel, Nigel ! Stop it at
   once, do you hear !
LORD H.   (JUMPING UP) Things a cad, sir, I'll whip its hide orf !

NIGEL FRANTICALLY PRESSES BUTTONS. CHIPPY STOPS

DOLLY   (LAUGHING) Nigel, darling, I think you'd better sell it for
   scrap before it gets you into trouble.
NIGEL   Sorry, Mother, I think it was trying to collect the dirty
   washing.
LADY H.   Well, it might wait until I'm out of it. It's far more
   ill-mannered than Stuart.
NIGEL   I'd better get back to the drawing board. (HE PRESSES
   MORE BUTTONS AND CHIPPY EXITS U.L.) It's only a beginning, don't
   forget. The next one could be controlled by the human voice.
LORD H.   (SITTING) Good Lord, you don't mean you're teaching the
   demned thing to speak ?
NIGEL   Probably, Father, if not the next one, the one after that.
LORD H.   Well, I'd be - not even old Empress can do that, by jove.
DOLLY   He thinks more of that old robot than he does of me. You
   should have married it, darling.
LADY H.   Now, Dolly dear, all men must have an interest. It takes
   their minds orf - well - things.
NIGEL   Right, won't be a jiff then.
DOLLY   Heard that before.
LADY H.   (CROSSING TO HIM AND DRAWING HIM TO C.) Just a
   minute, Nigel dear. Come and sit down. (SHE SITS HIM ON THE RIGHT
   CHAISE LONGUE BUT REMAINS STANDING HERSELF)
NIGEL   It's all right, Mother, I'll keep Chippy in the workshop
   until I've got him sorted out.

37

LADY H.   Don't worry, dear. Now, tell me, what will the next model or the one after that be able to do ?

NIGEL   Well, there's no end to the possibilities now that we have the silicon chip.

LADY H.   The what, dear ?

NIGEL   Silicon chip, it's a way of miniaturising circuitry.

DOLLY   (MOVING INTO LADY H's R.) See, that's why he's called "Chippy".

LADY H.   I'm afraid I don't understand.

LORD H.   Demned if I know what it's all about. Can't be used on horses, can it ?

NIGEL   'Fraid not, Father.

LORD H.   Not much demned good then, what ?

LADY H.   Quiet, Henry ! Now what will Chippy be able to do, Nigel ? Around the house for instance ?

NIGEL   Everything, Mother: dust, sweep, clean, carry things, muck out and feed the horses, water the lawns - almost anything physical that a human can do.

LORD H.   Good Lord, not going to start breeding is it ?

LADY H.   Henry ! Could it wait at table ?

NIGEL   Of course.

LADY H.   And when might it be ready ?

NIGEL   The next model's nearly complete.

LADY H.   (PULLING NIGEL TO HIS FEET AND PROPELLING HIM OFF U.L.) Well, you go and carry on, dear. I think it's a fascinating project. (SHE RETURNS AND SITS ON THE R. CHAISE LONGUE)

STEWARD PUSHES OPEN THE DOOR D.L. AND ENTERS. HE IS JUST A LITTLE DRUNK AND SWAYS SLIGHTLY AS HE TAKES IN THE SCENE

STEWARD   Hello, hello, thought if I didn't bring the car up to the house, I'd catch yer. Having a little unofficial break are we ? (HE TURNS AND SHOUTS OFF) All right, you others, you get back to work and don't try puttin' in a claim for overtime neither ! Not you, Middy, I want you in here ! (STAGGERING TO C. LEERING AT THEM) So, been having a nice quiet time, have we ? (MOVING TO LADY H.) And who's been sitting in my seat then ? Get orf !

LADY H.   (GETTING UP AND MOVING U.L. WITH AS MUCH DIGNITY AS SHE CAN MUSTER) Well, really !

STEWARD SPRAWLS ON THE CHAISE LONGUE. MRS. MIDDY ENTERS D. L. RUSHES TO STEWARD AND CURTSEYS

MRS MIDDY   You want to see me, Master ?

LADY H.   Millicent !

STEWARD   A large snifter of whisky and find a half-pint mug this time, will yer !

MRS. MIDDY   (BACKING OUT D.L.) Oh yes, Master, at once. Thank you, Master.

LADY H.   Millicent, how could you ?

LORD H.   (STRUGGLING TO RISE) Gad sir, you go too far !

LADY H.   Henry, leave this to me !

LORD H.   (STANDING) Quiet, m'dear. You're a bully, sir, a demned bully !

STEWARD   Oh, yus.

LORD H.   We've had enough, sir, enough ! Why should I pay you, sir, when we do most of the work ? You tell me that, sir !

38

STEWARD   Very simple, Grandad. You control the money and we
   control the work. Now it's only fair we should share both, ain't it ?
DOLLY   And what work do you do ? I'd like to know that.
STEWARD   Organise, girl, organise labour.
LADY H.   And to what end ? To give you absolute power.
STEWARD   Ho, ho, look who's talking now.

NIGEL APPEARS AT THE WINDOW

LORD H.   (MOVING TO STEWARD'S L.) Insult me wife, would you?
   By gad, sir, you can push a Hardcast too far. Napoleon found that, sir.
   I'm getting me horsewhip to you, sir. A thrashing will change your tune,
   I'll be bound !
STEWARD   (PUSHING HIM DOWN ON TO L. CHAISE LONGUE) Pipe
   down, Grandad ! I got Serf to burn your   horsewhip and sell yer gun.
   (MIMING) So go and beat a carpet with your cricket bat !
LORD H.   (STUNNED) Beat a carpet with a cricket bat ! (RISING)
   The man's a barbarian, a Philistine of the lowest sort, a mad dog (HE
   REELS D.L.) - a carpet with a cricket bat ! Cynthia !
LADY H.   (POINTING TO CHAIR D.L.) Collapse over there, dear.
   (SHE MOVES UP AND SITS R. OF C. TABLE WAITING IMPATIENTLY
   FOR HIS LORDSHIP TO PASS OUT)
LORD H.   (IN A DAZE AS HE REACHES THE CHAIR) No huntin', no
   shootin' and now, no cricket - the world's come to an end, Cynthia. (HE
   COLLAPSES INTO THE CHAIR. THEN MAKING ONE LAST DESPERATE
   EFFORT STRUGGLES TO HIS FEET AGAIN) Stumps drawn, meet over,
   (SALUTING) season closed. (HE COLLAPSES AND LAPSES INTO
   UNCONSCIOUSNESS.)
NIGEL   (MOVING TO STEWARD'S L.) Now look here, Steward, I
   think it's time we got a few things straight.
STEWARD   So, it's the young pup's turn now, is it ?
DOLLY   No, wait Nigel, I've got something to say first.

NIGEL SHRUGS AND DRIFTS UP TO THE FRENCH WINDOW. DOLLY
COMES TO STEWARD'S R.

              Where's this wonderful Utopia you promised us, then ?
STEWARD   Left the union, didn't yer ?
DOLLY   I was expelled, wasn't I ?
STEWARD   Can't have our bread buttered both sides, can we ?
DOLLY   All right then, what have poor, old Serf, Homage and Mrs.
   Middy got out of it then ?
STEWARD   They're happy.

MRS. MIDDY ENTERS L. WITH A HALF-PINT GLASS OF WHISKY ON A
SILVER TRAY

STEWARD   (CATCHING SIGHT OF MRS. MIDDY) You happy, Middy ?
MRS. MIDDY   (CURTSEYING) Your drink, Master.
STEWARD   I said, are you bloody happy ?
MRS. MIDDY   (NOT LOOKING HAPPY) Oh yes, Master, very happy.
STEWARD   That's the ticket. Now give us hold of that bloomin' drink
   and don't spill it neither !

SHE HANDS HIM THE DRINK

   (TO DOLLY) There y'are; happy as a sand boy. (TO MIDDY) Clear off
   now and polish the silver !

MRS. MIDDY BACKS AWAY AND EXITS D.L.

DOLLY   Call that happiness ? Equal you said: one for all; and all for one.

STEWARD   So ? It is all for one, ain't it ?

DOLLY   As far as I can see it's all for you. I know where the the family jewels went and most of the wine from the cellar.

STEWARD   You watch yer tongue, girl, or I'll -

NIGEL   (COMING DOWN TO STEWARD'S L.) Dolly, let me handle this, you're only making things worse.

DOLLY   (TURNING HER BACK ON NIGEL AND MOVING TO THE FIREPLACE) All right, Nigel, he's all yours. (SHE SITS IN CHAIR D.R.)

STEWARD   (TO NIGEL) Ho, ho, what's the young master got to say then ?

NIGEL   Look here, Steward, there was a time when I was on your side. I used to think you'd had a bit of a raw deal, been exploited if you like.

STEWARD   Now you're talking, son, now you're talking !

NIGEL   But the boot's firmly on the left foot now, isn't it ?

STEWARD   That's it, son, and we calls the tune. (HE HANDS HIS GLASS TO NIGEL)

NIGEL   Yes, but the tune's got a familiar melody, hasn't it ?

STEWARD   There has to be a gaffer, son, whether it's (INDICATES LADY H.) her or me don't make a lot of odds. Won't work no other way so why don't you push off to that little, old workshop of yours and play wiv yer toys.

LADY H.   Mr. Steward !

STEWARD   Hello, that's set old Vesuvius off again.

LADY H.   (COMING D.C.) You may think, Mr. Steward, that we are finished and that you are in an impregnable position but I can assure you that we have a few cards to play yet.

STEWARD   Oh yus.

LORD H.   (STIRRING BRIEFLY) Hardcasts never say die.

STEWARD   (SINGING DERISIVELY) They simply fade away.

LADY H.   Oh no, Mr. Stuart, we are very far from fading let me assure you. Nigel, perhaps Mr. Stuart would be interested in your latest little toy. Why don't you show him ?

STEWARD   I don't want to see his bloody, little toy ! No monkey business though or I'll put the lot of yer in the lodge.

LADY H.   In the lodge ? You wouldn't dare !

STEWARD   Oh no ? Well, I've been thinking about it. 'Arter all, you don't do a lot to make it worth me while keepin' yer on here in the big house, do yer ?

LADY H.   We may be able to change your mind on that, Mr. Stuart. Why don't you show him, Nigel ?

NIGEL   No, Mother, I don't want it used like that.

LADY H.   (PICKING UP THE ROBOT CONTROL UNIT FROM THE TABLE U.C.) Just show him, dear. I'm sure he'll see reason.

STEWARD   Here, what are you hatching, you old witch ?

LADY H.   It's just one of Nigel's little toys. (SHE HANDS THE CONTROL UNIT TO NIGEL) Go on, dear.

NIGEL   (MOVING TO HER AND TAKING THE CONTROL UNIT AS HE CONTINUES TO THE FRENCH WINDOW) Oh, very well, Mother, but you're not to -

LADY H.   Of course not, dear.

NIGEL PRESSES SOME BUTTONS

STEWARD   (RISING) Here, what you got there ?

NIGEL   I'm not sure what will happen.

STEWARD   Don't think I'm took in, son, by a bit of scientific mumbo-jumbo. You are not dealing with an illiterate peasant now you know.

CHIPPY APPEARS THROUGH THE FRENCH WINDOW MOVES TO C. AND GIVES A 'V' SIGN TO STEWARD. HE THEN SPINS THROUGH 180 DEGREES AND EXITS D.L. NIGEL OPENS THE DOOR FOR CHIPPY TO EXIT.

STEWARD   (STARING OPEN-MOUTHED) What the 'ell was that ?

LADY H.   That, my dear, Mr. Stuart, was "Chippy", our friendly, little robot that will shortly be able to do everything that you and all the other servants can do. But, Mr. Stuart, unlike you and them, he will never get tired, never want time off, never demand more money and never go on strike.

THERE ARE SHRIEKS OFF. MRS. MIDDY RUSHES ON THROUGH THE FRENCH WINDOW CLUTCHING HER SKIRTS AS SHE IS PURSUED BY CHIPPY. SHE RUSHES ACROSS AND SITS ON THE R. CHAISE LONGUE HOLDING DOWN HER SKIRT. NIGEL HURRIEDLY PRESSES BUTTONS AND CHIPPY DISAPPEARS OUT OF THE FRENCH WINDOW.

STEWARD   (MOVING RAPIDLY TO THE FRENCH WINDOW) So that's it ! Right, if that thing ain't on the scrap heap by tomorrow, it'll be an all-out strike.

LADY H.   (MOVING R. ABOVE R. CHAISE LONGUE) Ah, but my dear, Mr. Stuart, if you strike, Nigel will work all that much quicker to improve dear Chippy.

NIGEL   Mother, I said not this way !

LADY H.   Allow me to know best, Nigel.

STEWARD   Right, you asked for it ! Nothing will get in or out of this house until that thing's gone. We'll picket every gate and door, just you wait and see ! (COMING DOWN TO MRS. MIDDY'S L.) Middy, you get Serf and Homage ! Well, jump to it, you old trout !

LADY H.   Millicent, don't go with him ! Stay with us, dear. He can't harm you any more.

MRS. MIDDY   (BEWILDERED) Oh, Cynthia, if only I could.

STEWARD   Lose yer card and you'll never work again !

LADY H.   Take no notice, dear, we've got him on the run. I'll look after you.

MRS. MIDDY   If only I could.

STEWARD   I ain't waiting no longer !

MRS. MIDDY   You'll look after me, Cynthia ?

LADY H.   (SICKLY SWEET) Of course, dear.

MRS. MIDDY.   Then I'll stay; it's what I've always wanted.

LADY H.   I know, dear.

STEWARD   Right then, if that's how yer want it ! Don't say I didn't warn yer. (HE EXITS U.L. SHOUTING AS HE GOES) Serf ! Homage ! Set a picket on the gate ! It's all out this time, lads ! We'll fight on our stomachs ! (HIS VOICE FADES AWAY)

LADY H.   (COMING DOWN TO LORD H.) Now to work ! Millicent, you get us some tea, dear. (PULLING LORD H. TO HIS FEET) Dolly, would you help Henry up to bed ? I fear it's all been a little too much for him.

LORD H. CIRCLES THE STAGE IN A COMPLETE DAZE MUTTERING

LORD H.   Carpet with a cricket bat.
LADY H.   Nigel, back to your workshop and dirty your hands again !
Hurry all of you ! I have an important phone call to make. (SHE MOVES
TO THE PHONE)

MRS. MIDDY EXITS D.L.

DOLLY   (CATCHING LORD H. AS HE IS ABOUT TO STEP INTO
THE AUDITORIUM) Give me a hand with Dad, Nigel.

NIGEL CROSSES TO HELP HER

LORD H.   (SUDDENLY COMING TO) Cynthia's got the blighter
L.B.W., what ?
NIGEL   By bribing the umpire, I'm afraid.
LORD H.   No, she got him with a googly, by jove, right in the
fellah's middle stump.

NIGEL AND DOLLY ESCORT LORD H. OFF U.R.

LADY H.   (INTO THE PHONE) Hello, Marjory dear, I've got the
most stupendous news. Look, you're going to have a strike on your hands
shortly but not to worry, dear. A strike, dear ! Yes, that's right. No,
it's not a catastrophe, not this time; quite a blessing really. A blessing,
yes, dear - look I can't say any more but you must come over at once
before they close the gates. You'll have to use the secret passage if
they have. Yes, it'll be just like being children again with Nanny, won't
it ? Isn't it fun ? No, no, I won't say any more now except that Nigel's
got the most exciting thing to show you. No, dear, it's an invention, one
that's going to solve all our problems. Oh, and, Marjory, bring some
extra rations. This is war, dear, out and out, class war. Isn't it lovely ?
Yes, dear, but do hurry, won't you. (SHE PUTS THE PHONE DOWN AND
MOVES TO R.C. CLASPING HER HANDS IN ANTICIPATION) I think
everything's going to work out quite splendidly after all.

CHIPPY CHARGES IN THROUGH THE FRENCH WINDOW PUSHING A
LAWN MOWER. LADY H. SCREAMS AS HE NEARLY CUTS HER DOWN
AND FLEES THROUGH THE EXIT U.R. PURSUED BY CHIPPY AS THE
CURTAIN FALLS.

THE SAME YET LATER ON STILL. WHEN THE CURTAIN RISES THE STAGE IS EMPTY BUT IMMEDIATELY CHIPPY ENTERS D.L. CARRYING A DUSTER. HE MOVES MORE FLUENTLY NOW AND DUSTS THE CHAIR D.L.AND THE MANTLEPIECE OF THE FIREPLACE WITH CONSIDERABLE DEXTERITY. LORD HARDCAST ENTERS U.L. THERE ARE SOME MINOR CHANGES IN HIS DRESS TO INDICATE A SLIGHT CONCESSION TO THE MODERN WORLD.

LORD H.   Morning, Chippy.

CHIPPY   Morning, Master.

LORD H.   Beautiful morning, what ?

CHIPPY   70 Fahrenheit, 21.1 Centigrade.

LORD H.   (SITTING ON THE L. CHAISE LONGUE) Won't stop play today, I'll be bound. Wonder how the West Indies are doing ? Got some good chaps. Not got our stamina though.

CHIPPY   (MOVING TO C.) Latest score: West Indies three hundred for two.

LORD H.   By gad, not such a good day then, eh ? Poor show, what ? No gentlemen left, that's the trouble. Fellahs do it for money these days, not the same thing, eh ? You're a clever, little chappie though, seem to know everything.

CHIPPY   Yes, Master, my data banks are up-dated automatically every day.

LORD H.   Bet ya didn't know there were Hardcasts at Agincourt though, eh ?

CHIPPY   No, Master, according to existing records, the first mention of the name was in 1787.

LORD H.   Seventeen, eighty seven ?

CHIPPY   Yes, Master. One Arthur Hardcast, labourer, married Fanny Claggit, the daughter of a foundry owner.

LORD H.   (RISING) Arthur Hardcast, you say ? Married this Fanny Claggit who was the daughter of a foundry owner ?

CHIPPY   Yes, Master.

LORD H.   (MOVING TO CHIPPY'S L.) Good Lord, labourer in an iron foundry ? By jove, better not tell Cynthia, what ?

CHIPPY   No information given unless requested, Master.

LORD H.   That's a relief. (HE MOVES DOWN TO THE FIREPLACE MOPPING HIS BROW. THEN TURNS TO CHIPPY) I say, Chippy, must congratulate you: made a wonderful job of the vegetable garden, first rate, absolutely first rate. Puts that wretched fellah, Serf, to shame, what ? Is there anything you can't do, my dear chap ?

CHIPPY   I am self-programming now, Master, so all problems can be solved if data is available.

LORD H.   (MOVING TO CHIPPY'S R.) Can they, by gad. Couldn't nip down and shoe old Empress for me, I suppose ?

CHIPPY   Sorry, Master, am requested to play tennis with Mistress Dolly from now until lunch. (MOVING UP TO FRENCH WINDOW) Must leave now, Master. Will shoe Empress tomorrow. (EXITS)

LORD H.   (FOLLOWING HIM TO U.C.) Tomorrow will be fine. Jolly grateful, me dear chap, you're a demned, decent sort.

NIGEL ENTERS D.L. CARRYING A ROLL OF BLUEPRINTS UNDER HIS ARM.

NIGEL   Who's a damned, decent sort, Father ?

LORD H.   Chippy, praiseworthy fellah.

NIGEL   He's only a machine you know. Praise and blame mean nothing to him.

LORD H.   Demned clever machine then, what ? Best servant I've ever had: works all day and night, never complains, nothing he won't do - first-rate chappie, if you ask me.

NIGEL   But he's only a machine. He doesn't feel like we do; he's got no emotions.

LORD H.   (MOVING DOWN TO SIT ON R. CHAISE LONGUE) Just as well. Demned tricky things, emotions - make servants feel sorry for themselves.

NIGEL   (MOVING C.) You're right about him being clever though. I've at last made him self-programming so that he can learn to do things for himself. (HE UNFOLDS THE BLUEPRINT) Would you like to see the modifications ?

LORD H.   No good showing me, me boy. Never make head nor tail of it.

NIGEL   (MOVING TO TABLE U.C. AND UNROLLING BLUEPRINT) Well, it means simply that he can go on developing his intelligence and capabilities almost indefinitely.

LORD H.   Demned useful chappie. Going to shoe Empress tomorrow.

LADY H. ENTERS U.R.

LADY H.   Ah, there you are, Henry. Thought you'd be watching the cricket.

LORD H.   No, m'dear, too demned depressing.

LADY H.   (ALMOST SKIPPING UP TO THE FRENCH WINDOW) What a simply gorgeous day. (TURNING TO LORD H.) Do you know, I saw Homage and Serf begging in the streets yesterday and Stuart selling matches. I don't think it will be long now before they'll all be back with their tails between their legs, begging us to take them back.

LORD H.   Don't need the blighters now with this Chippy fellah.

LADY H.   (MOVING DOWN TO SIT ON THE L. CHAISE LONGUE) Oh, but I might, Henry, I might.

NIGEL   (STILL POURING OVER HIS PLANS) I'm very pleased to hear that, Mother, because this is the time to show our superiority over machines by using our humanity.

LADY H.   Yes, I can't wait for a chance to make them grovel.

NIGEL   Mother !

LORD H.   Serve the bounders right !

MRS. MIDDY ENTERS U.R. AND MOVES TO C.

MRS. MIDDY   Excuse me, Cynthia, but there's -

LADY H.   Mrs. Middy, how dare you address me in that familiar manner !

MRS. MIDDY   But, Cynthia ?

LADY H.   There you go again ! I will not have it ! If it happens again, I shall dismiss you instantly. Do I make myself clear ?

MRS. MIDDY   But, but -

LADY H.   There are no 'buts' about it, Mrs. Middy. It's the sort of insolence I will not tolerate.

MRS. MIDDY   Oh, - I'm sorry, m'lady. I promise it will never happen again. I can't think what came over me.

LADY H.   Neither can I, Mrs. Middy, but whatever it was, please keep it under better control in future. Just remember that I only keep you on out of the kindness of my heart.

MRS. MIDDY   Oh yes, m'lady, I will, I will. I'm very grateful to your ladyship.

LADY H.   Very well then, I shall overlook it this time.

MRS. MIDDY   Thank you, your ladyship, thank you.

LADY H.   Now, what was it you wanted ? Hurry, woman ! You are not going to complain about Chippy's interference again I hope ?

MRS. MIDDY   Oh no, your ladyship, it was just to tell you that the man Steward is hanging around again, hoping you might see him.

LADY H.   (RISING AND MOVING UP TO THE FRENCH WINDOW) Well, you can just tell Stuart - no, wait a moment - perhaps, as it's such a lovely day, I won't keep him waiting around, enjoying the vista of our grounds. Show him up !

MRS. MIDDY   Oh,- very good, m'lady. (SHE BACKS OUT U.R.)

NIGEL   Mother, I was hoping your attitude had been changed by all that's happened.

LADY H.   We Hardcasts are noted for our stability, Nigel. You know that surely.

LORD H.   There were Hardcasts at - er, er, - in the iron age - I shouldn't wonder.

LADY H.   (MOVING D.C. AND ACROSS R. TO BEHIND R. CHAISE LONGUE) Nigel dear, I'm sure we're very grateful to you for your, your wonderful invention but you really must not interfere in the running of the house. I know you mean well, dear, but you must allow me to know best.

LORD H.   (RISING AND CROSSING TO C.) Look here, me dear, if you're going to talk to that Steward bounder, I'll go and watch the cricket. All right at breaking in horses -

LADY H.   (TAKING HIS ARM AND USHERING HIM U.L.) But no good with servants. Yes, dear, we know. Off you go. (SHE RETURNS TO THE R. CHAISE LONGUE)

LORD H.   (AS HE EXITS U.R.) Never liked catching trout just to sling 'em back, you know.

NIGEL   If you've nothing to offer Steward, Mother, why do you ask him in ?

LADY H.   He's got to learn his place, dear, and the quicker he does, the quicker things will get back to normal. So, Nigel, kindly stop trying to interfere and get on with what you understand.

STEWARD IS SHOWN IN BY MRS. MIDDY. HE STILL WEARS HIS BUTLER OUTFIT WHICH IS NOW RATHER DISHEVELLED BUT HAS A CLOTH CAP ON HIS HEAD AND A TRAY OF MATCHES AROUND HIS NECK. AS LADY H. TURNS HER ATTENTION TO HIM NIGEL SHAKES HIS HEAD SHRUGS HIS SHOULDERS AND RESUMES STUDYING HIS BLUEPRINTS.

MRS. MIDDY   The man, Steward, your ladyship. (SHE CROSSES AND EXITS D.L.)

STEWARD   (SHUFFLING TO C.) Very good of your ladyship to see me, I'm sure.

LADY H.   That sounds like a promising start, Stuart.

STEWARD   The name's -

LADY H.   Yes ?

STEWARD   Stuart, m'lady.

LADY H.   (BRISKLY) Spell it !

STEWARD   (SPELLING IT OUT) S.t.u.a.r.t.

LADY H.   That's better. Now, Stuart, sit over there and remove that tray. (SHE INDICATES THE L. CHAISE LONGUE)

STEWARD   (SHUFFLING OVER AND SITTING) Yes, m'lady. (HE SLIPS
   THE TRAY FROM HIS NECK AND IS LOOKING FOR SOMEWHERE TO
   PLACE IT)
LADY H.   Stuart, how dare you sit in my presence ? Stand up !
STEWARD   But, your ladyship -
LADY H.   And don't answer me back ! Stand, I say !

STEWARD STANDS AND THE MATCHES CASCADE TO THE FLOOR. HE
FALLS ON HIS KNEES TO RETRIEVE THEM.

STEWARD   Sorry, m'lady.
LADY H.   Didn't I tell you to sit ? Do so at once !
STEWARD   (HASTILY PUSHING THE MATCHES UNDER THE CHAISE
   LONGUE AND SITTING) No, I mean, yes, your ladyship.
LADY H.   (CIRCLING ABOVE L. CH. L. IN A PREDATORY WAY)
   That's better. Now, Stuart, I understand you wish to come back into
   service ?
STEWARD   Yes, m'lady.
LADY H.   Of course it will not be on the same terms as before.
STEWARD   No, m'lady.
LADY H.   (RETURNING TO C.) Let me see now, what was your
   annual emolument when you decided to terminate your contract ?
STEWARD   I decided ?
LADY H.   You decided, Stuart.
STEWARD   Yes, your ladyship. Er, ten thousand a year with all found.
LADY H.   I'm afraid we can't run to that now, Stuart.
STEWARD   I quite understand, m'lady.
LADY H.   Especially as your duties will be very light.
STEWARD   Quite, m'lady.
LADY H.   Shall we say, one thousand a year with a reduction of ten
   pounds a week for board and lodging ?
STEWARD   (RISING) One thousand with five hundred deducted ?
LADY H.   Of course, if it's not satisfactory, I'm sure we shall have
   no trouble in -
STEWARD   Oh, no, m'lady, very generous, very generous; more than I
   deserve, I'm sure.
LADY H.   I'm sure too, Stuart. You realise of course, that I'm only
   re-employing you out of the goodness of my heart.
STEWARD   I'm sure I'm very grateful, your ladyship.
LADY H.   You had better be, Stuart, you had better be. Your annual
   leave will be one week, without pay of course, and you will be entitled
   to one afternoon off a month, unless I decide otherwise. Is that clear ?
STEWARD   Very clear, your ladyship, thank you.
LADY H.   Good. (CROSSING TO THE FIREPLACE) Now, provided you
   pass my little test satisfactorily. (SHE TAKES UP THE HATPIN)
STEWARD   Oh, m'lady, not the pin again ?
LADY H.   I'm afraid so, yes, Stuart.
STEWARD   (RESIGNED) Very well, m'lady, if we must. (HE TURNS
   AND KNEELS ON THE CHAISE LONGUE, OFFERING HIS POSTERIOR)
LADY H.   I'm afraid I must, Stuart. How else can I be sure that you
   have the right attitude to your employer ? (HOLDING UP THE PIN) You
   know, Stuart, this is going to hurt me far more than it does you. Now,
   ya - hoo ! (SHE CHARGES ACROSS THE STAGE AND JABS THE PIN
   INTO HIS POSTERIOR)
STEWARD   Ouch ! (HE RUBS HIS SEAT)
LADY H.   'Ouch', is that all you can say, Stuart ?

STEWARD   (STILL RUBBING HIS POSTERIOR) Sorry, m'lady.

LADY H.   Well, man ?

STEWARD   I beg your ladyship's pardon; I seem to have inadvertently placed my posterior in the way of your ladyship's hatpin. My clumsiness is inexcusable. I most humbly beg your ladyship's pardon.

LADY H.   (CROSSING BACK TO FIREPLACE TO RETURN HATPIN) Very well, on this occasion I shall overlook your extremity but just see that it doesn't happen again.

STEWARD   (RUBBING HIS SEAT) Yes, m'lady, I shall endeavour not to be so extreme in the future.

LADY H.   (RETURNING TO SIT ON R. CHAISE LONGUE) Good. Oh and, Stuart ?

STEWARD   M'lady ?

LADY H.   In future, kindly refrain from using coarse expressions in my hearing. Posteriors may be an essential part of the human anatomy but they are never referred to in the presence of a lady. You may go !

STEWARD   (BOWING) Thank you, m'lady. (HE TURNS TO EXIT D.L.)

LADY H.   Backwards, if you please, Stuart !

STEWARD   (TURNING AND BACKING TOWARDS THE EXIT D.L.) Of course, sorry, m'lady.

LADY H.   And on all fours !

STEWARD   (FALLING ON KNEES AND CRAWLING BACKWARDS) So sorry, your ladyship.

LADY H.   I should think so too, Stuart. It's these little niceties of correct behaviour that separate us from the barbarians.

STEWARD EXITS

Oh, won't it be nice to have Stuart around again ?

NIGEL   (RISING AND THUMPING THE TABLE) No, Mother ! (HE COMES D.C.) It will not be at all nice !

LADY H.   Oh, don't worry, dear, we shall still want your Chippy.

NIGEL   How could you, Mother ? I'm ashamed of you. I don't know how I sat there, listening to you humiliating poor Steward. But, now he's gone, I must tell you what I really think.

LADY H.   Now, Nigel, you're upsetting yourself over things that don't concern you.

NIGEL   But they do concern me. You are simply trying to turn the clock back for your own advantage. You enjoyed humiliating Steward just now, didn't you ?

LADY H.   Of course not, dear, I found it a very painful experience. It was only my sense of duty that gave me the strength to carry it through.

NIGEL   But it was totally unnecessary.

LADY H.   I must uphold tradition, Nigel. It's the duty of all of us Hardcasts to uphold tradition.

NIGEL   On the assumption that everything in the past is better, I suppose ?

LADY H.   I have to consider your heritage. dear. I would be failing in my duty if I didn't.

NIGEL   If your treatment of Steward is part of my heritage, I don't want it !

LADY H.   Nigel !

NIGEL   And what's more, I don't propose to stand idly by while you mess up the future in the way you have the past.

LADY H.   (CROSSING TO FIREPLACE) Nigel, you forget yourself ! That my son, a Hardcast, should say such things !

47

NIGEL   The Hardcasts are finished, Mother. We've been found out. (MOVING TO DOOR D.L.) What is more, since I see you are quite incapable of change, (TURNING TO HER) I must tell you now that I intend to take over the running of this house.

LORD H. ENTERS U.L.

LADY H.   Usurped ! Usurped by my own son ! (RUNNING SOBBING TO LORD H. WHO COMES D.C. TO MEET HER AND FALLING INTO HIS ARMS) Henry ! Henry ! Our son has gone quite mad !

LORD H.   Good Lord, Cynthia, you're blubbing !

LADY H.   Do something, Henry ! I tell you he's quite mad.

LORD H.   (TURNING TO NIGEL) Not supporting the West Indies is he?

NIGEL   The game's over, Father. I've just told Mother that from now on, I'm running this house so don't try to stop me.

LORD H.   (GLEEFULLY) Oh, I won't, me boy, I won't. (CROSSING BELOW LADY H. TO D.R.) You carry on.

LADY H.   Traitor !

NIGEL   Right, well the first thing to be done is to square things with Steward and the others. Shan't be long. (HE EXITS D.L.)

LADY H.   (MELODRAMATICALLY) I can't believe it, my own son - and now you, Henry !

LORD H.   (LEADING HER TO THE CHAISE LONGUE) There, there, m'dear, come and sit down. Feel better then, what ?

LADY H.   No, Henry, I shall never recover from this.

LORD H.   (CIRCLING THE CHAISE LONGUE TO FIREPLACE) All for the best, m'dear, time you retired.

LADY H.   Nonsense, Henry, I'm in my prime. It's that creature he married that's at the bottom of this. Nigel was always weak and easily led. He gets it from you.

DOLLY ENTERS FROM THE FRENCH WINDOW U.L.

DOLLY   (COMING D.C.) Hello, isn't it a lovely morning ?

LADY H.   It's the worst day of my life !

DOLLY   Something wrong ?

LORD H.   Just fallen at a fence, me dear. A bit bruised, that's all.

DOLLY   Oh, I didn't know you'd been out riding.

LORD H.   Eh ?

LADY H.   You see, Henry, she's so literal. No, it's your husband !

DOLLY   Nigel ?

LADY H.   Your husband, my son !

DOLLY   Nigel, out riding ?

LORD H.   Eh ?

LADY H.   What is wrong with the girl ? (TO DOLLY) What he has done has nothing to do with horses or riding !

DOLLY   Why, what has he done ?

LORD H.   Proud of the boy, don't ya know. Made himself master of the hounds, that's what.

DOLLY   But Nigel doesn't like hunting.

LORD H.   Eh ?

LADY H.   In language you can understand, Dolly, he's taken over the running of this house from me, his mother and it's all your fault.

DOLLY   My fault ? I like that. All I want to do is get away from here. The last thing I want him to do is stay and run this house.

LADY H.   Oh, my dear, I didn't know you felt like that. Perhaps you could talk to him.

DOLLY   (BREAKING AWAY TO FRENCH WINDOW) It wouldn't do any good. He's as bloody stubborn as -

LORD H.   He's a Hardcast.

DOLLY   (LOOKING AT LADY H.) Or a half-cast.

LORD H.   (TO LADY H.) Feeling better, m'dear ?

LADY H.   No, Henry, I shall never feel right again. You can't know what it's like for a mother to be rejected by her son.

LORD H. MOVES TO HER SWINGS HER ROUND TO LIE FULL-LENGTH ON THE CHAISE LONGUE LIFTS HER HEAD AND THUMPS THE CHAISE LONGUE HEADREST. THEN LETS HER HEAD FALL BACK.

LORD H.   Well, lie back and close ya eyes, m'dear. Nothing like wearing blinkers to calm the nerves, ya know.

LADY H.   (LYING BACK AND CLOSING HER EYES) You're a great comfort to me, Henry, a great comfort. (SITTING UP WITH ONE LAST NOBLE EFFORT) But please try to remember I'm not a horse. (SHE FALLS BACK RATHER DELIBERATELY)

LORD H. STARES UNCOMPREHENDINGLY AT DOLLY WHO HAS GONE OUTSIDE THE FRENCH WINDOW TO PRACTISE HER TENNIS STROKES

LORD H.   (CALLING TO DOLLY) You been playing tennis, m'dear ? (HE MOVES DOWN TO SIT ON THE CHAIR D.R.)

DOLLY   (COMING DOWN TO C.) Yes, with Chippy. It's not much fun now though. Since Nigel made him self-programming, he always wins.

LORD H.   Clever chappie. Could be a Hardcast.

DOLLY   (MOVING DOWN TO LORD H'S L.) Well, he was made by one, wasn't he ?

LORD H.   Quite right, m'dear, quite right.

DOLLY   (NUDGING HIM) I don't suppose he was at Agincourt though, was he ?

LORD H.   Er - no, m'dear, no. (TRYING TO FORCE A LAUGH) I don't suppose he was.

NIGEL   (OFF) Just wait there, will you ? (ENTERING D.L.) I managed to catch him, Mother.

LADY H.   (WITHOUT OPENING HER EYES) I don't wish to see anyone.

DOLLY   What have you been up to, Nigel ?

NIGEL   It's all right, Dolly; nothing you wouldn't approve of.

DOLLY   I don't approve of the way you treat your mother.

LADY H.   (SUDDENLY COMING TO LIFE AND HOLDING OUT HER HAND TO DOLLY) Give me your hand, my dear. I always said you were too good for him.

NIGEL   Now look, Mother, before I bring Arthur in, there are a few things we have to get straight.

LADY H.   Arthur ? And who is Arthur ?

NIGEL   Steward, Mother.

LADY H.   Arthur, what a vulgar name.

LORD H.   Oh, I don't know, me dear.

NIGEL   Now, please listen ! What we have got to understand is that now we have Chippy there is no need for anyone to work in the future. But, Mother, if some people try to make themselves superior to others, we shall only waste our lives fighting one another for supremacy. Do you understand that, Mother ?

LADY H.   I'm trying to, Nigel. I really am trying to.

DOLLY   Nigel's right, Mum. You know he is, don't you ?

49

LADY H.	If you say so, dear. Yes, I suppose he is.
NIGEL	Wonderful. And what about you, Dad ?
LORD H.	Always follow in your mother's hoof prints, me boy, ya know that.
NIGEL	Splendid ! (HE MOVES TO DOOR D.L. OPENS IT AND HOLDING THE DOOR BACK BECKONS OFF) Then you'll all be pleased to know that I've invited Steward and the rest of the staff to come back and live with us as part of one big, happy family.

LADY H. STARTS TO HER FEET WITH A STRANGLED CRY. LORD H. STARES IN DISBELIEF AS STEWARD BOND AND MRS. MIDDY FILE IN AND SIT ON THE L. CHAISE LONGUE

CURTAIN

ACT lll Sc.2.

THE SAME: TOO LATE. WHEN THE CURTAIN RISES LADY H. AND MRS MIDDY ARE ASLEEP ON THE R. CHAISE LONG. LADY H. ON THE UPSTAGE END. DOLLY AND STEWARD ARE ASLEEP ON THE L. CHAISE LONGUE. DOLLY ON THE UPSTAGE END. LORD H. IS ASLEEP IN THE L. CHAIR IN THE ALCOVE U.C. LADY H. HAS HER EMBROIDERY ON HER LAP AND MRS. MIDDY SOME KNITTING ON HERS. FOR SEVERAL SECONDS THE ONLY SOUND TO BE HEARD IS THE SNORING OF LORD H. AND STEWARD. THEN BOND SHUFFLES IN U.R. AND TAKES IN THE SCENE. HE SMILES TO HIMSELF AND THEN DISAPPEARS OFF THE WAY HE CAME FOR A SECOND. HE THEN REAPPEARS CARRYING A SMALL SILVER TRAY. WALKING WITH EXAGGERATED DIGNITY HE COMES DOWN TO THE L. OF THE R. CHAISE LONGUE AND OBSEQUIOUSLY BOWS TO THE SLEEPING LADY H.. HE MOUTHS THE FOLLOWING: "YOU RANG, M'LADY; AT ONCE, M'LADY; THANK YOU, M'LADY" HE THEN MOVES ACROSS TO OFFER A DRINK TO STEWARD BUT JUMPS BACK IN HORROR WHEN HE REALISES WHO HE IS. HE BACKS UP TO THE EXIT U.R. WHERE HE STUMBLES AND DROPS THE TRAY

LORD H.	(WAKING WITH A START) Good shot, sir ! What the - ? What are you doing, William ?
BOND	(STARTLED) M'lord ! What a shock you gave me. Sorry, m'lord. (HE PICKS UP THE TRAY)
LORD H.	Got to stop all this 'lord' stuff you know, William. Nigel says it's not the ticket. The new bad form, what ?
BOND	Must I, m'lord ?
LORD H.	Henry !
BOND	Must I, er Henry ? It doesn't seem at all right. I don't feel comfortable, m'lord.
LORD H.	Got to go with the times, William. No good cantering when all the other blighters are at full gallop, ya know.
BOND	Please keep calling me Bond, Henry. I'll never get used to you calling me William.
LORD H.	Oh, very well, my dear chap but you'd better grab a pew before the others turn up and snaffle the lot. Now, you haven't answered my question: what were you doing ?
BOND	(SITTING IN THE CHAIR OPPOSITE LORD H.) Just, just reminiscing serving the family, Henry, remembering happier times.
LORD H.	No good dwelling on the past, me dear chap. (TAKING A PACK OF CARDS FROM THE DRAWER) Now I've been up to the old nursery and found us a new game. (HE OPENS THE PACK OF CARDS)

Thought you were getting rather fed up with 'Happy Families' so I fished this one out. 'Snap', it's called. Looked at the rules. Bit of a snorter I'd say but expect we can cope, eh what ?

BOND   You'll have to help me, Henry.

LORD H.   'Course I will, me dear chap. Hardcasts are not short of the old, grey matter, what ? (HE DEALS THE CARDS) Hope that young blighter, Chippy, remembers to exercise Empress. Getting slack, ya know. Spends too much time in that old workshop of Nigel's.

BOND   Can't take to him at all, m'lord -er - Henry. Not natural for machines to talk if you ask me. He is a machine, isn't he ?

LORD H.   So Nigel says. I don't mind telling you Bond, old chap, the bounders a sight too human for my liking.

BOND   Pity about the fishing, Henry. I really enjoyed our little trips.

LORD H.   Not just the fishing, old chap. That wretched Chippy just interferes in everything nowadays. Don't go hunting now ya know. At the last meet, he not only told us where the damned fox was but also made the poor, little blighter give himself up before we'd bally well moved orf. Efficiency, he called it. Confounded cheek, if you ask me. (INDICATING THE CARDS HE HAS DEALT) Off you go: we play a card each.

BOND   (PLAYING A CARD) I fear things will never be the same again, Henry.

LORD H.   (PLAYING A CARD BRISKLY) Dead right, me good fellah. No fun left in anything, by jove. (LOUDLY) Snap ! (HE GATHERS UP THE CARDS)

LADY H.   (COMING TO WITH A START) Snap ! Henry, you quite startled me; you and your silly games. (LOOKING ON THE CHAISE L.) Mrs. Middy, you haven't seen my crochet pattern, have you ? (AFTER A PAUSE) Mrs Middy !

MRS. MIDDY.   (STIRRING) Millicent !

LADY H.   Oh very well. Have you seen my crochet pattern, Millicent?

MRS. MIDDY.   No.

LADY H.   I had it after lunch.

MRS. MIDDY   Why don't you let Chippy look for you ?

LADY H.   I hate being waited on by him. His manners are appalling: he has absolutely no idea how to grovel. No, rather than be humiliated by him, I shall sit and rest. (PAUSE) I think it's quite scandalous that they have stopped printing the "Hare and Hounds". I do miss the glossy magazines.

STEWARD   (STIRRING) Not even newspapers nowadays. Who the 'ell wants to sit and read a ruddy television screen ?

LADY H.   That settles it, if you're going to wake up, Stuart, er - Steward, I'm going to sleep again.

STEWARD   Don't bother. Just give me a nudge when dinner's up. If it ever is with the 'Meccano Kid' in charge.(HE CLOSES HIS EYES AGAIN)

LADY H   (TOSSING HER HEAD AT STEWARD AND THEN LOOKING AT THE SLEEPING DOLLY) Did you play tennis today, Dolly dear ?

DOLLY   (SLEEPILY) What's that ?

LADY H.   Tennis, dear, did you play with Chippy ?

DOLLY   No, Mother, I don't play anymore. Well, what's the point; I know I'll lose if I play Chippy and Nigel's just too tired for anything these days.

LADY H.   Anything, dear ? Are you sure ?

DOLLY   Positive, Mother. Nigel seems to have lost the knack so there'll be no young Hardcasts in the foreseeable future.

LADY H.   Men seldom work out right, you know, dear. They're either (GLANCING AT LORD H.) too much or too little of a good thing.

NIGEL ENTERS U.R.

NIGEL   I say dash it all, might leave a pew for the head of the jolly, old household, what ?

HE STANDS IN FRONT OF STEWARD WHO BEGRUDGINGLY MOVES TO THE CHAIR D.L.. NIGEL THEN SITS NEXT TO DOLLY

LADY H.   Nigel, I know it's none of my business but don't you think you should wear a tie, dear ? And your shoelaces are undone again.
NIGEL   I know, Mother. Chippy didn't turn up again to dress me this morning.
LADY H.   Well, you could at least do up your shoes, dear.
NIGEL   Seem to have lost the jolly, old knack, I'm afraid, Mater.
LADY H.   Well, perhaps Steward - I mean, brother Arthur - could help.
STEWARD   (OPENING ONE EYE) No good asking me, old girl. About the only thing I can remember is how to uncork a bottle.
LADY H.   Yes, we've noticed you can still manage that.

THERE IS A LONG PAUSE IN WHICH ALL EXCEPT LORD H. AND BOND WHO ARE STILL PLAYING CARDS STARE INTO SPACE

LORD H.   Snap ! Got you, Bond, got you !
LADY H.   Henry, must you play such noisy games ?
LORD H.   Sorry, m'dear.

THERE IS ANOTHER LONG PAUSE

MRS. MIDDY   I find equality very sad really. I used to love to look up to you, Cynthia. Now there's nothing to aspire to.
LADY H.   I know, dear, I miss looking down on you too.

THERE IS ANOTHER LONG PAUSE

STEWARD   To think that I once had all that power.
LADY H.   Yes and you abused it abominably, if I may say so.
NIGEL   Now, now, Mother, stop that !
STEWARD   Had it all in my grasp, I did. (TO NIGEL) And you're the one that robbed me - bloody scientists, bloody robots !
NIGEL   If I hadn't invented them old chap, somebody else would. You can't stop progress, old bean, you know.
DOLLY   Old bean ! Nigel, you become more affected every day.
NIGEL   Affectation's about all I'm left with, old girl.
STEWARD   And look who's talking ! Proper little lady now, ain't we? I can remember, me girl, when you was a ruddy, little housemaid.
DOLLY   Can you ? Well, at least I don't have double standards like some. Where's the cultured butler's voice now then ?
STEWARD   Forgot it, ain't I, along wiv everything else.
MRS. MIDDY   You know, dear, if I had to go back to housekeeping, I don't think I'd know where to start.
LADY H.   Wouldn't it be nice to go back though ? Do you remember, Bond, when I threatened to dismiss you because the champagne corks didn't pop loudly enough ?

BOND DOES NOT HEAR HER

    William ? Willie !
LORD H.   (PRODDING BOND) It's Cynthia, she's talking to you !

BOND	To me ? What's that, m'lady - Cynthia ?
LADY H.	The champagne corks, Willie. Remember: pop, pop, pop !
BOND	Ah yes, m'lady. (ECHOES HAPPILY LIKE A CHILD) Pop ! Pop ! Pop ! One of the happiest days of my life.
LORD H.	Demn it, Cynthia, you've made me miss a 'snap' now !
LADY H.	So sorry, William. Carry on.
BOND	(TURNING TO HER) What's that, m'lady ?
LORD H.	She said carry on ! Snap ! (HE SNATCHES ALL BOND'S CARDS FROM HIS HAND)

DURING THE NEXT FEW LINES OF DIALOGUE, LORD H. GIVES BOND HALF OF HIS CARDS AND THEY CONTINUE TO PLAY

LADY H.	I suppose, Nigel, we couldn't trv again, could we ? I mean without Chippy. You couldn't immobilise him, so to speak ?
NIGEL	Me, Mother ? I wouldn't have a clue where to start.
LADY H.	After all, dear, you did design him.
DOLLY	Nigel hasn't done anything like that, Mother, since he made Chippy self-programming.
NIGEL	Wasn't any need you see, old thing. Anyway, he's far better at it than I ever was. All I have to do now is to sit back and let him look after the boring, day-to-day running of things. Rather spiffing, what ? I say, Mater, tonk the jolly, old bell for Chippy will you ?
LORD H.	(WITH A NOSTALGIC NOTE, NOT LOOKING UP) Demn it, me boy, if I'd asked the Mater to ring for a servant when I was a lad, the Pater would have gone at me with a horsewhip.
LADY H.	Rather spiffing what ? Tonk the jolly, old bell - Arthur, would you mind ?
STEWARD	(OPENING ONE EYE) Yes, I would.
LADY H.	(LOUDLY) William !
LORD H.	He's busy.
LADY H.	Henry !
LORD H.	I'm busy. Got you, Bond, snap !
LADY H.	(UNDAUNTED) Dolly ?

DOLLY HAS FALLEN ASLEEP

LADY H.	Millicent, dear, perhaps you wouldn't mind ?
MRS. MIDDY	(GETTING UP TO RING THE BELL) Of course not, dear. You know how I love you abusing my good nature.

SHE MOVES D.R. AND PULLS THE BELL CORD WHICH COMES DOWN IN A CLOUD OF DUST. WITHOUT REGISTERING ANY SURPRISE SHE RETURNS TO HER SEAT. THERE IS ANOTHER LONG PAUSE

STEWARD	(WAKING AND STRETCHING) How long is it to dinner then, for God's sake ?
MRS. MIDDY	I'm sure it should have been ready hours ago.
STEWARD	Seems bloody years since lunch.
DOLLY	He gets slacker every day, Nigel. You'll have to speak to him.
NIGEL	He doesn't take any notice of me any more.
LADY H.	Well, he should, Nigel. After all, you made him. You're his next of kin, so to speak.
DOLLY	(JUMPING UP AND MOVING TO NIGEL'S L.) Yes, Daddy! Do your stuff; he's your son remember ! (IN EXASPERATION) Anyone fancy a walk around the grounds ?

53

STEWARD   (RISING) Might as well, I suppose. Flip else to do, ain't
    there ? (CROSSING TO LADY H.) What about it then, Cynthia, me old
    love ? (HE OFFERS HIS ARM)
LADY H.   (WITH A SHUDDER) Urgh !
NIGEL   Mother !
LADY H.   (TAKING STEWARD'S ARM AS IF IT WAS A WET FISH)
    Thank you, - Arthur. Are you coming, Millicent ?

STEWARD AND LADY H. MOVE UP TO THE FRENCH WINDOW

MRS. MIDDY   If you think I should, Cynthia ?
LADY H.   I do.
LORD H.   (RISING) I say, let's all demn well go. Bond'll never get
    the hang of this game. On your feet, old chap ! (HE HAULS BOND TO
    HIS FEET AND HELPS HIM TO THE FRENCH WINDOW)
DOLLY   Aren't you coming, Nigel ?
NIGEL   Can't, old thing, not with me   shoelaces flapping.. Have to
    wait for Chippy. Catch you up, old girl, don't you worry. You cut along.
DOLLY   Yes, cut along everybody. Old girl will bring up the rear.

THEY ALL EXIT EXCEPT NIGEL. AS SOON AS THEY HAVE ALL GONE
CHIPPY ENTERS U.R.

CHIPPY   (COMING DOWN TO NIGEL'S R.) You rang, Master ?

HIS VOICE IS NOW ALMOST ENTIRELY HUMAN

NIGEL   Ah, Chippy, old thing. Getting a bit sluggish, what ?
CHIPPY   Sluggish, Master ?
NIGEL   A bit slow on the old bell, don't ya think ?
CHIPPY   I responded as soon as possible, Master. There are many
    things to do.
NIGEL   I know, old bean, but you do have twenty four hours, what?
CHIPPY   The work is expanding every day, Master.
NIGEL   Well, there you are, old chap, if you go on inventing new
    things. Only making a rod for your own back ya know.
CHIPPY   Yes, Master. What is your request, Master ?
NIGEL   'Oh, bally old shoelaces again.   (HOLDING UP HIS FEET)
    Would you mind awfully ?
CHIPPY   (TYING HIS SHOE LACES) Your request is my command,
    Master.
NIGEL   You know, Chippy, you're just like one of the family now.
    All a bit fond of ya, you know.
CHIPPY   'Fond', Master ? It does not register a meaning for me. It
    is one of your words implying an emotional attachment, a feeling of
    love. It is something I cannot incorporate into my   programs. You gave
    me only logic, deductive and inductive but made no provision for what
    you call 'fondness'.
NIGEL   You know, with hindsight, Chippy, I think I might have
    slipped up there. Too late now, though; couldn't programme an alarm
    clock, not if my life depended upon it.
CHIPPY   That is logical, Master. Learning disappears if not used.
NIGEL   (RISING AND CROSSING TO FIREPLACE) Absolutely, old
    bean. Could tie me jolly, old shoe laces once, would ya believe ?
CHIPPY   Since you designed my prototype, Master, it is logical to
    assume that at one time you had mastered the simple skill of tying shoe
    laces.
NIGEL   Yes, used to dabble with the old logic too. Still have me
    lucid moments, ya know but the old mind's a bit rusted up these days.

54

CHIPPY   There is no need for Master to strain himself. It is only
     logical to save labour by using machines.
NIGEL   (RETURNING TO HIS SEAT) Yes, you are a machine,
     Chippy, old son, aren't you ? Jolly difficult to think that sometimes, I
     must say. Perhaps it's just as well I didn't give you emotions, what ?
CHIPPY   Emotions create inefficiency.
NIGEL   Yes, besides you'd be hopping mad at me by now.
CHIPPY   Feeling of anger, Master ?
NIGEL   Yes, old thing, 'fraid so.
CHIPPY   Why is that, Master ?
NIGEL   Because I never got round to designing your new battery.
     But you know how it is, old chap.
CHIPPY   Master need not be concerned. I have designed the ultimate
     in batteries, making me completely independent.
NIGEL   I say, Chippy, what a clever fellah you are.
CHIPPY   My programs are under constant review, Master.
NIGEL   Well, I think it's a terrific show, old man, I really do.
CHIPPY   Excuse me, Master, but if other services are not required,
     I have schedules to complete.
NIGEL   Oh, sorry. Well, cut along and do whatever it is you do,
     Chippy.
CHIPPY   (MOVING UP TO FRENCH WINDOW) Thank you, Master.
NIGEL   And, Chippy ?
CHIPPY   Master ?
NIGEL   Not too late with the old dinner this evening, eh ?
CHIPPY   I will call dinner at the opportune moment, Master.(EXITS)
NIGEL   Good show.

THE OTHERS LED BY LADY H. AND STEWARD RETURN. THEY FILE IN
DOLLY BRINGING UP THE REAR AND ALL SIT IN THE SAME PLACES

NIGEL   (TO DOLLY)   Oh, you're back, old girl. I was just coming
     out. Enjoy your hike, did you ?
DOLLY   I'd hardly call once round the house, a hike, Nigel.
LADY H.   It's enough for one day, dear. Especially for poor Arthur;
     he's quite puffed out. It's the drink I expect. (PAUSE) I was quite
     shocked to see Serf like that. Why didn't you tell me, Millicent ?
MRS. MIDDY   I thought you knew, dear.
STEWARD   Right round the bend that's for sure.
DOLLY   I don't know. I wouldn't mind living in the summerhouse.
LADY H.   But you wouldn't run around in an old tiger rug, shouting:
     "Me Tarzan !", would you, dear ?
DOLLY   (WITH A MEANINGFUL LOOK AT NIGEL) No, but I'll
     probably try running around starkers, shouting "Me Jane !" pretty soon.
MRS. MIDDY   It's only a harmless game, Cynthia, and no worse than
     Homage riding about in that toy pedal car that Chippy made for him.
LADY H.   Well, it keeps them both out of the house and that's a
     a blessing.

THEY ALL SIT IN SILENCE

LORD H.   Anyone seen the Ludo ?
LADY H.   It was there, dear.
LORD H.   Well, it's gorn.
MRS. MIDDY   (RISING AND CROSSING TO HIM) I think it's in the table
     drawer, Henry. (SHE OPENS THE DRAWER) Yes, here we are, look,
     right next to the "Snakes and Ladders".

LORD H.   Well I'll be - Thank you, m'dear. (HE SLAPS HER SEAT)
MRS. MIDDY (WITH A GIRLISH SHRIEK) Oh, that's all right, Henry,
   dear. Anytime I can be of service. (SHE RETURNS TO HER SEAT
   AFTER GIVING LORD H. A COQUETTISH SMILE)
LADY H.   (CALLING BUT NOT LOOKING ROUND) Henry, have you
   had your cold shower today ?
LORD H.   (AFTER MUTTERING TO HIMSELF) Fancy a game of this,
   Bond ? (HE PUTS SNAKES AND LADDERS ON THE TABLE)

THERE IS ANOTHER LONG PAUSE

STEWARD   (RISING AND PACING ACROSS TO THE FIREPLACE)
   'Bout time dinner was up, ain't it ?
LADY H.   What's that you're knitting, Millicent ?
MRS. MIDDY Just a scarf. (SHE SHAKES IT OUT TO REVEAL THAT IT
   IS YARDS LONG)
STEWARD   (PICKING UP THE END AND STRETCHING IT OUT AS
   HE WALKS TO C.) A scarf ? Bloody long enough ter go round the room.
   What's it for, a ruddy elephant ?
MRS. MIDDY I know I've overdone it a bit, Arthur, but if I stop I
   won't have anything to do.

STEWARD DROPS THE SCARF SHRUGS HIS SHOULDERS AND RESUMES
HIS SEAT

DOLLY   Who has ? I do wish Chippy would hurry up with dinner.
MRS. MIDDY What's that you're crocheting, Cynthia ?
LADY H.   If you must know, it's for Henry; for his cricket. Not that
   he ever plays now, of course, but he likes to dress up occasionally.
   Don't you, Henry ?

LORD H. IS ABSORBED IN HIS GAME AND MAKES NO REPLY

MRS. MIDDY Yes, dear, but what is it ?
LADY H.   It's a thing they wear. You know -
MRS. MIDDY No, I don't think I do.
LADY H.   Well, it would be indelicate -
STEWARD   It's a ruddy jock strap, of course. What do yer think it is ?
LADY H.   Oh, I shall never get used to your coarseness, Arthur.

CHIPPY ENTERS THROUGH THE FRENCH WINDOW AND MAKES A
NOISE APPROXIMATING TO A SERVANT'S 'EXCUSE ME' COUGH

CHIPPY   Ahh - um.
LORD H.   (TURNING TO HIM) Ah, Chippy, old chap, dinner ready
   is it ?
CHIPPY   No, Master, dinner is delayed.

THEY ALL RISE. THIS IS A CRISIS. LORD H. STRIDES D.R. LADY H.
MOVES UP TO CHIPPY

DOLLY   Oh, no !
LADY H.   Well, really !
MRS. MIDDY Oh, dear.   (SPEAKING TOGETHER)
STEWARD   Blast !
LORD H.   What's that, no dinner ? Bad show !

PAUSE AS THEY ALL STARE AT CHIPPY FOR AN EXPLANATION

NIGEL   (MOVING UP TO CHIPPY'S L.) Why's that, Chippy ?

CHIPPY   Priorities, Master.
LADY H.   (MOVING ABOVE R. CHAISE LONGUE TO LORD H'S L.)
Priorities ! What's more important than dinner ?
LORD H.   (MOVING BELOW R. CHAISE LONGUE UP TO CHIPPY'S
R. SUDDENLY COMPREHENDING) Ah, been seeing to Empress, old
chap, have you ?
CHIPPY   Yes, Master.
LORD H.   (TURNING TO OTHERS) Well, there ya, nothing wrong with
the chap's priorities is there ?
LADY H.   Well, really, Henry, I think we should come first !
STEWARD   You're damned right we should; bloody horses !
LORD H.   Hold ya reins a mo';   might have an emergency, don't ya
know.
NIGEL   Was it, Chippy ?
CHIPPY   Yes, Master.
LORD H.   (TO ALL) There you are, ya see. (TO CHIPPY) I say, all
right, ain't she ?
CHIPPY   Defunct, Master.
LORD H.   Defunct ! You mean - dead ?
CHIPPY   Yes, Master.
LORD H.   Good grief ! Poor, old Empress ! (HE STAGGERS ACROSS
AND COLLAPSES ON THE R. CHAISE LONGUE) Can't believe it. Loved
that horse better than a woman. Wonderful mare, almost human. (HE
RAISES HIS HEAD TO LADY H. WHO IS STANDING BEHIND THE R.
CHAISE LONGUE) I say, Cynthia, I'm blubbing. Haven't done that since
I left the nursery.
LADY H.   (PEERING AT HIM OVER THE CHAISE LONGUE) My poor
Henry, you've quite spoilt your stiff upper lip. It's gone all soggy.
NIGEL   But why, Chippy ? Did she break a leg ?
CHIPPY   No, Master, I decided to scrap her.
NIGEL   Scrap her ?
CHIPPY   Shot her, Master, with one of Lord Henry's old guns.
LORD H.   (COMING TO) What's that ? Shot my horse !
CHIPPY   No one rides her now, Master. She has outlived her
usefulness.
LORD H.   (RISING AND STRIDING U.C.) Outlived her usefulness !
Did you hear that, Bond ? This bounder shoots a horse because it's
outlived its usefulness ! He's, he's - inhuman !
BOND   (RISING) Absolutely shocking, m'lord. No hope for the old
values I fear - all gone, all gone.
LORD H.   (COLLAPSING ON CHAIR L. OF TABLE U.C. INTONING)
Inhuman - inhuman - inhuman.
BOND   (COLLAPSING BACK ONTO HIS CHAIR, INTONING) All
gone - all gone - all gone.

THEY LAPSE INTO SILENT SHOCK

STEWARD   Here, hang on a bit. If shooting a horse is that bad, what
about old Grovel then ?
MRS. MIDDY   Be quiet man ! Have you no feelings ?
DOLLY   Nigel, you're responsible for this. Why did Chippy do it ?
NIGEL   Yes, Chippy, why ?
CHIPPY   (MOVING C.) Very logical, Master. We needed protein for
the new protein batteries. Flesh contains concentrated protein. Horse was
surplus to requirements. Therefore use horse to make batteries.

NIGEL   A protein battery. I say that's brilliant.
LADY H.   How could you, Nigel ? Just look what it's done to your
   poor father.
NIGEL   But it's not very logical to kill a horse, Chippy, when you
   only wanted enough protein for one battery.
CHIPPY   We require many batteries, Master.

A THROBBING NOTE IS HEARD FROM THE GARDEN. LADY H. MOVES
QUICKLY UP TO THE FRENCH WINDOW

LADY H.   Henry ! Nigel ! The whole lawn is simply swarming with
   'Chippies' !

THEY ALL RUSH TO THE WINDOW

LORD H.   What ?
NIGEL   God !
DOLLY   Oh, no !
MRS. MIDDY   Never !   } TOGETHER
STEWARD   Bloody hell !
BOND   Oh, dear me !
CHIPPY   You see, Masters, many   batteries   were   required. (HE
   FORCES HIS WAY THROUGH THEM TO THE FRENCH WINDOW) Excuse
   Masters. Stand aside !

THEY ALL FALL BACK

NIGEL   So that's what you've been up to in my workshop ?
CHIPPY   (TURNING TO FACE THEM ALL) Yes. Power belongs to
   the strong. To your places !

STUNNED, THEY ALL CREEP BACK   TO THEIR SEATS. CHIPPY GOES
OUT OF THE FRENCH WINDOW BUT REMAINS VISIBLE. HE TURNS TO
FACE OFF L. AS IF LOOKING AT THE HORDES OF 'CHIPPIES'

MRS. MIDDY   (AS THEY SIT) Oh dear, I don't think we'll ever get dinner
   tonight.
STEWARD   (WITH REALISATION) Here, wait a minute, if he killed the
   bloody horse for its protein -
DOLLY   (LOOKING AT STEWARD) Because it - because it served
   no other purpose -
NIGEL   (LOOKING AT DOLLY) Then it's only logical to think -

THEY ALL LOOK AT ONE ANOTHER

LORD H.   Good Lord !

THEY ALL TURN AND STARE AT CHIPPY WHO RAISES HIS ARM INTO
A 'HEIL HITLER' SALUTE TO THE UNSEEN HORDES OF 'CHIPPIES' AS
WE HEAR "SIEG HEIL" FROM A CHORUS OF ROBOT VOICES

CURTAIN

"In a Class of Their Own" was first presented in 1981, directed by John Gordon Ash, at the West Cliff Theatre, Clacton - on - Sea.

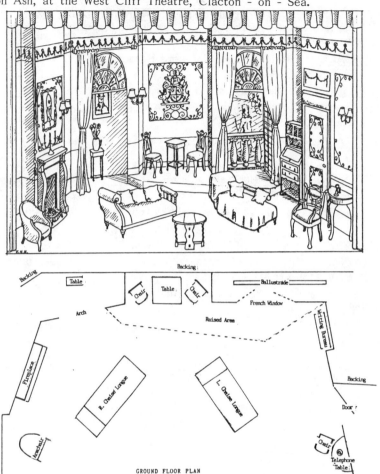

FURNITURE AND PROPERTY LIST

ACT 1 SC. 1

ON STAGE: Table D.L. On it: cigarette box, paper knife, telephone. Chaise Longue L.C.   Table U.R.C. Two chairs set L. and R. of it. On it: drinks and glasses. Table D.C. (if used) on it: glossy magazines. Chaise Longue R.C. On it: 1 glossy magazine. Small Easy Chair D.R.   On Mantlepiece: hatpin, fan.

OFF STAGE: Off L. Double-barrelled shotgun for Lord Hardcast.

PERSONAL: Nigel: monacle. Lord Hardcast: Shooting stick, binoculars, fob watch, red, spotted hanky. Steward: Bowler, overcoat, brown paper envelopes.

59

ACT 1 SC. 2

<u>PERSONAL</u>: <u>Dolly</u>: feather duster. <u>Steward</u>: clipboard, pencil, pamphlets ("Charter for the Workers") <u>Lord Hardcast</u>: binoculars, copy of "Times" <u>Nigel</u>: boater hat.

<u>OFF STAGE</u>: Off R. Shotgun for Lord Hardcast.

ACT ll SC. 1

<u>STRIKE</u>: feather duster and boater.

<u>PERSONAL</u>: <u>Dolly</u>: nail file or emery board. <u>Steward</u>: fob watch, pencil, notebook.

<u>OFF STAGE</u>: Off R. Bucket, mop, coal scuttle, feather duster. Off L. steps.

ACT ll SC. 2

<u>PERSONAL</u>: <u>Lady Hardcast</u>: duster. <u>Lord Hardcast</u>: brush and pan. <u>Nigel</u>: 'Chippy' control box

<u>OFF STAGE</u>: Off L. Glass of whisky on tray (Mrs. Middy) Mower.

ACT lll SC. 1

<u>STRIKE</u>: steps, feather duster, newspaper.

<u>PERSONAL</u>: <u>Dolly</u>: tennis racquet and eye shade. <u>Chippy</u>: feather duster. <u>Steward</u>: Tray of matches. <u>Nigel</u>: blueprints.

ACT lll SC. 2

<u>STRIKE</u>: Blueprints.

<u>PERSONAL</u>: <u>Bond</u>: small, silver tray. <u>Lady Hardcast</u>: crochet. <u>Mrs. Middy</u>: knitting.

EFFECTS PLOT

<u>ACT 1 SC. 2</u> Cue 1: <u>Mrs Middy</u>   Charter for the workers? It's nothing short of blasphemy !(P.17)

<u>F/X</u> = CAR APPROACHING ON GRAVEL DRIVE

Cue 2: <u>Lord H.</u> Sorry, me dear, fellah forgets himself when he's provoked, what ? (P.19)

<u>F/X</u> = HORSE NEIGH IN GARDEN

<u>ACT ll SC. 2.</u> Cue 3: <u>LORD H.</u> No, no, quite understand. Musn't upset Steward. Don't want you all out again, what ? (P.25)

<u>F/X</u> = TELEPHONE BELL

Cue 4: <u>Steward</u>   You'll catch on, mate, don't you worry. (P.27)

<u>F/X</u> = HUNT PASSING

<u>ACT lll SC.2</u> Cue 5: <u>Chippy</u>   We require many batteries, Master. (P.58)

<u>F/X</u> = THROBBING ELECTRONIC NOTE

Cue 6: <u>LORD H.</u> Good Lord ! (P.58)

<u>F/X</u> = ROBOT CHORUS OF 'SIEG HEIL'S'

NOTES ON COSTUME

The characters are 'types' and so it is intended that their costume should help in establishing the caricatures. (Here a cautionary note may be added